COMMUNICATION SKILLS TRAINING

A 4-Step Guide To Boosting Your Charisma And Persuasion Skills. How To Improve Empathy And Assertiveness In Your Daily Conversations

POSITIVITY FOCUSED TEAM

Introduction

"The most basic of all human needs is the need to understand and the need to be understood. The best way to understand people is to listen to them." – Ralph Nichols

So, when we think of communication, we, like most other people, tend to look for ways in which we can impart knowledge, rather than take it in. Think about it. When you are thinking of communication, you really only think about speaking. In fact, even when you are thinking about listeners, you think of them in the context of speakers, as they exist solely to support speaking.

But that doesn't really make sense, does it? If listeners only have value when there is a speaker, isn't it the same for a speaker? Aren't they also worthless on their own?

And yet, great orators and speakers are lauded and rewarded, whereas listeners are considered to be superfluous to the entire experience.

This is because in modern history, mainly Western history, the emphasis has always been on the individual who commands the crowd. This is why when communicating we believe that the only way to connect is to speak, but in doing so, we are overlooking a key element—our audience.

Who are we speaking to?

What are they doing?

What should they be doing?

Right?

Wrong.

Hold up and rewind for a second. Did you notice that while you were going through this whole passage, you immediately mentally assigned yourself as the speaker and thought of X, Y or Z as the listener? Why do you think that is?

Well, frankly, it's because of power—the concept of being the person in control of a crowd rather than being one of the people who is being controlled makes you feel like you are more authoritative and better than your listener. This brings us to the next issue—respect. Because listeners are deemed to be 'weaker,' you also mentally categorize them to be less worthy of your respect. This in turn totally offsets the communication balance and makes your communication very one-sided.

Let's start by fixing this.

Before you focus on what another person should be doing, or what you think they need to do, why not first focus on building your own communication skills? Before you go off and try to teach other people how to listen to you, why not learn how to listen to others?

Think you're up for the challenge?

Great!

What we're going to learn right now is called Active Listening. Active listening is a technique that attunes you to the speaker so that you are not only focused on the speaker's words but also their body language. This is critical as non-verbal communication can play a crucial role in terms of verifying the authenticity of the information that you are receiving.

The goal of active listening is to ensure that as you are spoken to, you genuinely try to take in the information that is being provided. Think of it like this— if your mom is asking you to get her a sheet of paper so she can note something down while she is on the phone, and you come back with only a sheet of paper, have you actually listened?

What if I said—no?

The key issue in her statement was that she wanted the sheet of paper so she could take a note. Now ask yourself, is a blank sheet of paper going to be useful without a pen or pencil?

You see, listening is about more than words registering in your mind, it's about understanding the intent and purpose conveyed by those words so that you can help facilitate a solution based on those cues. There are many techniques you can use to enhance your listening skills. Since you are just beginning, why don't we start with nine necessary steps that can help?

So, are you ready to become a Master Listener?

Awesome!

Here we go!

Technique 1: Offering Support

Have you ever wondered why you feel comfortable saying things to some people and uncomfortable saying things to others? Why do you think that is? Well, it's because some people have indicated to you, either overtly or subliminally that you are safe with them, and that you can confide in them and that you are being taken seriously. Now, if you feel like that when you are speaking, and if someone who is just listening can make you feel comfortable or uncomfortable, don't you think you have the ability to do the same when you're the listener?

So, how can you do that?

Scenario One:

Let's say that, you are a professor, and you have an exam to conduct in roughly ten to fifteen minutes. At this time, your colleague who has been having a rough time with management has come to you to speak about the issue because they believe you can help them.

You want to help them, and you want to hear them out, but you're looking at the hall clock every two minutes and are slowly inching toward the classroom as you nod distractedly to their tirade.

How do you think your colleague feels?

Do you think they feel heard?

The odds are they don't, and that's understandable. You would feel the same.

Well, let's go back and evaluate what went wrong. When your colleague came to talk to you, you knew two things. (a) That you have a class in ten minutes, and (b) that they wished to converse with you on a topic that was going to take more than ten minutes. The problem was that both of these issues are incompatible, which means that by saying nothing, you are putting yourself in an impossible position. Not only are you not going to get to class on time at this rate, but you also won't be able to make your colleague feel like you valued their time or shared their concern. In short, they will have felt cut off and unsupported.

What you just did was "passive" listening. Your role as a listener was inert and did not respond to the circumstances. So, what would "active" listening look like in this case?

Well, to begin—active listening assesses.

So, when your colleague came to discuss the problem, as an active listener, you would've realized you didn't have enough time to finish the conversation right now.

So, if you had told your colleague you had a class in ten minutes and as this was an important issue that would take longer than the ten minutes you could spare now, you would have expressed that although you wish to help them, you can't at this moment.

Then, for good measure, if you added a suitable time when you are free, you'd be actually putting in a concentrated effort. Not only would you be telling them that they matter, verbally, but you would be using an action to follow up that behavior.

Now, you can get to class on time, and your colleague doesn't think you're apart! Win-win!

Technique 2: Creating Openings

So, have you ever felt claustrophobic?

You know, when you feel everything was closing in on you? When there was just too much pressure bearing down on you, and you needed to get up and be able to get away? Well, that is another common side effect of bad communication.

You see, communication needs to be liberating. When you as a listener, aren't making your speaker feel safe and secure, your speaker will have a harder time explaining what the problem is and will be more inclined to lie or to put on an act.

With good communication, you can make your speaker feel like there is a large berth between the two of you, not one that keeps you away from them, but one that gives them room to breathe, and not feel like they are being interrogated by the Spanish Inquisition.

Basically, you need to encourage them to speak, but you also need to enable them to make a choice. So, give them an opening, but don't grab them by the collar.

Let's give things a little context, shall we?

Scenario Two:

Your boyfriend, Clark has had a rough day. He used to be a high flyer with a great job, but after this new company called Stark Enterprises moved in, he lost his job. He has been unemployed for months, and this evening upon coming home from work, you notice that the house is a mess and he has red-rimmed eyes.

Which of the following should be your response?

Response 1: Clark, what's wrong? Are you upset about the job?

Response 2: Hey Babe, it's been a rough day hasn't it? Shit happens; you'll get better opportunities.

Response 3: Hey Babe, the house is nuts. Why don't we get dressed and grab dinner outside, and we can deal with this stuff later?

Response 4: Hey you, are you okay?

In Response one you are basically cornering your boyfriend. Clark now feels very much like you've put him on the spot and is automatically going into a defensive mode where he is feeling like an underperformer because you mentioned his lost job. He has to pretend otherwise because you already suspected that the behavior could be due to his loss of a job.

You won't get anywhere with that, and in instances like Response two, where you steamroll through his answer, don't really help either. So, what should you do?

Response three ignored the entire premise and tries to change the topic to something lighter like dinner plans. The problem with that though, is now Clark feels like his troubles aren't important enough to merit a conversation, and you can't be

12

bothered to talk about it which is why you are both mentally and physically avoiding the issue.

The ideal response is Response four, where you have shown a good amount of interest and indicated that you are open to a conversation should Clark wish to have one. But you have not been specific enough to let on that you know something is wrong, giving Clark control to now either tell you or avoid the issue.

Pretty cool, eh?

Chapter 1. The Importance of Communication Skills

Developing your communication skills can help all aspects of your life from your professional life to social gatherings, and everything in between. The ability to communicate information accurately, clearly and as intended, is a vital life skill and something that should not be overlooked. It's never too late to work on your communication skills and by doing so, you may well find that you improve your quality of life.

To demonstrate just how important good communication is. I've listed some of the benefits it can have on your professional life.

In Demand by Businesses, oral and written communication proficiencies are consistently ranked in the top ten desirable skills by employer surveys year after year. Employees are often encouraged to take online courses and in-person training to improve their presentation and communication skills.

It Improves Team Building. Honest and effective communication can create a strong team. When staff consults with each other, consider other opinions, and discuss their progress, they will be more enthused to collaborate. As a result, the strong unit that they create makes the workplace more enjoyable, and they will be eager to perform well so they don't let their teammates down. Indeed, communication helps solve employee morale issues by keeping entire teams in the loop, making all team members feel useful within the workplace. This lack of secrecy not only boosts team spirit, but it also has a positive effect on staff attitudes.

It Boosts Growth. Great communication contributes to the growth of the business, which goes hand in hand with your career. It eliminates uncertainties and speeds up the process of policies to ensure there is a smooth delivery of projects. Take eCommerce website Zappos, for example: their ethos relies on great communication within the organization and with their clients – something that earned them a spot on Fortune magazine's 2015 list of the 100 best companies to work for.

Helps your career progression. You will need to request information, discuss problems, give instructions, work in teams, and interact with colleagues and clines. If you are to achieve cooperation and effective teamwork, good human relations skills are essential. Also, as the workplace is also becoming more global, there are many factors to consider if you are to communicate well in such a diverse environment. Being able to deliver messages clearly and understand other people means work can be completed more effectively and to the benefit of the company as a whole. Employers want staff who can think for themselves, use initiative and solve problems, staff who are interested in the long-term success of the company. If you are to be seen as a valued member of the organization, it is important not just to be able to do your job well, but also to communicate your thoughts on how to processes and products or services can be improved.

It allows you to speak concisely. It is natural to feel some nerves when speaking to superiors or to clients. Communication skills training will help you learn how best to communicate effectively in a wide range of situations, and how to be direct in order to get the most out of your dealings with others.

Build Better Rapport with customers. Customers desire nothing more than to be understood by a company and they wish to feel like they are being heard and listened to. This is a particularly important point if your business involved a large amount of contact with customers, either face-to-face or over the phone.

Influences how you learn. Communication skills have played an important part of your existing knowledge and beliefs. You learn to speak in public by first having conversations, then by answering questions and then by expressing your opinions. You learn to write by first learning to read, then by writing and learning to think critically. Good communication skills help you absorb information and express your ideas in a clear, concise and meaningful way to other people.

Enhances your professional image. You want to make a good first impression on your friends and family, instructors, and employer. They all want you to convey a positive image, as it reflects on them. In your career, you will represent your business or company in spoken and written form. Your professionalism and attention to detail will reflect positively on you and set you up for success.

It increases innovation. If employees are scared of communicating their thoughts and ideas out of fear of being rejected, then they are likely to become stagnant in their career and only contribute the bare minimum. However, if there is an open line of communication between supervisors and staff members, they are encouraged to be more creative and innovative within the workplace, and they are likely to put forth new and creative ideas. In today's fast-moving workplace, most ideas are likely to be pushed under the carpet due to a lack of communication. As Cisco managing director Alex Goryachev writes on Forbes: "People listen mostly to respond rather than to understand. However, digitization demands active listening to the ecosystem in order to survive and develop collaborative strategies with startups, partners, and costumers around the world".

Managing Diversity in the workforce. Good communication is even more important if the workforce is diverse. With a mix of races, nationalities, genders or faiths on the job, it is easy for people to accidentally offend each other. If promotion and employee review rules aren't clear, minority workers may feel they've been discriminated against. Policies clearly spell out how the company applies rewards and penalties can clear things up. Clear guidelines telling employees how to treat each other helps avoid unwanted conflict.

It improves productivity. Being able to communicate effectively at work can help increase overall productivity. Managers can understand their employee's talents and skills and will then give clear directions to the people that are best suited for the job, thus increasing the overall turnaround time of any given project. For example, one colleague may be faster and better at using Excel than others; therefore, through communication, a manager can identify this and task them with managing the spreadsheets. If there was a lack of conversation, meanwhile the project would suffer, and the entire process would slow down, negatively affecting the goal of the company as a result.

It increases efficiency. Poor communication compromises efficiency, as well as the overall quality of work. When instructions aren't provided clearly, mistakes are bound to happen. On the other hand, clear instructions eliminate the need to clarify and correct any issues. Think back to a time where you didn't communicate well with a colleague. It probably resulted in wasted time, effort, and resources. So, if you happen to have a manager that doesn't communicate effectively, make sure you ask the right questions to get the information that you need successfully complete a project. Over time, they will understand what they should be supplying you with so you can start working on your tasks.

It increases loyalty. When you have a good line of communication with management, you're naturally going to be more loyal to the organization. You will feel comfortable discussing any professional or personal issues, and you'll be more committed to the company. This free line of communication also builds trust between a manager and an employee which results in a loyal relationship. A two-way line of respect ensures that there is no micromanagement involved and that an employee is trusted to get on with the job that they were hired to do.

It reduces mitigation conflict. Two people in the workplace may feel that they are communicating well but because they both have different methods of communication; they are misunderstanding each other. Therefore, working with different personalities requires excellent communication skills to limit any conflict in the workplace. If you are experiencing conflict at work, it's important to look beyond the issue at hand and identify the other person's thought process. You need to consider the communication pattern of the receiver to get a better understanding of what they are trying to say.

It increases employee engagement. Good communication goes far beyond talking: it's more about connecting and engaging with others. When teams are engaged, they are more aligned with the company's goals and are generally more motivated to work towards the set targets. It's also easier for managers to identify what makes a positive and satisfying working environment, allowing them to work towards achieving a balanced working life for their employees.

It resolves problems. There's bound to be characters that clash and opinions that differ within any working environment. And what's the best way to solve those problems? Clear communication! Effective communication isn't about who's right and wrong: it's about having an open, honest and positive discussion to ensure everyone's needs are met! You're not always going to see eye to eye with your work nemesis but if you can find a way to work well with them, you'll make the environment much more enjoyable for everyone around you!

It enhances skills. Managers can identify hidden talents when they communicate clearly with their employees. By doing so, they can tap into these skills, and help enhance them, which will contribute to the overall success of the business. For example, John may be hired a customer service representative, but through conversation, his manager identifies that he has previous experience in marketing. John is then transferred to marketing and is much better suited at the position. If the lack of communication were there, however, John would have become stagnant later down the line, and the business would have lost a great talent.

In every aspect of your job, you'll be required to communicate in one way or another. It's important to understand just how valuable effective communication is and what impact it can have on your relationships and your progression within the working world.

Chapter 2. Listening is as important as Talking in Communication

Our brains and our technologies are hardwired to work against us when it comes to listening. First, you have your heuristic brain patterns constantly seeking shortcuts to better understand information so that you can tune out and move on. You also have the brain networks that control your judgment. This area refuses to accept novel information, ideas, and people that don't fit comfortably into your current mental models. Add to that technology constantly pinging away at your attention span. Open listening comes from an open and focused mind. Clearly, you have a lot stacked against you. But don't worry, we are going to heighten your sense of awareness and practice self-restraint.

Truly listening to someone has become outmoded. This is a very good thing. Becoming a great listener is your surefire way to stand out, gain attention, and significantly increase your likelihood of crafting communications that resonate with the person you are speaking with.

The best way to learn how to listen is by learning how to avoid not listening, since listening itself is fairly straightforward. The following are the three main enemies to good listening. Shutting them off is your key to success. When you begin falling into one of these three traps, slap your brain out of it. After all, it's not in control here—you are.

Don't Formulate a Response, Ever

Becoming a great listener can be extremely difficult if you like talking a lot. We can't help ourselves—we want to jump in and add to the conversation. Well, now is the time to stop that for good. Each time your brain starts articulating a response as someone else is talking, give yourself a mental slap. Slap all of the nonsense out of your brain and keep it open to the words coming at you. Focus on those words.

Avoid Sentence-Grabbing and Sentence-Cutting

Want to make someone dislike you? Cut them off midsentence. Or even worse, hijack a word or phrase someone says and begin talking about that instead. It will veer the entire conversation in a different direction, thereby ensuring that you missed the message. Also, it will expose you for what you are: a jerk.

Every time we communicate, we are attempting to express a piece of ourselves in some way. Don't hijack someone's moment or cut them off at the knees. It's bad for you and them. Stop that thought. Slap it away and stay focused.

Shut Down Brain Biases, Judgments, and Conclusions

This is the trickiest habit to practice because you're going to have to recognize behaviors happening back in the mainframe computing sections of your brain. You probably don't even realize they are happening. In fact, there are hundreds of them and when they take over, your brain stops listening. The first set of programs is called heuristics: well-intentioned shortcuts our brains make to produce a judgment. Then there are biases, which are shortcuts our brains take to jump straight to a conclusion without hearing all of the information. The following is an exercise for shutting those programs off, which must be done if we are to become great listeners.

Suspend Your Beliefs

Imagine that you're listening to someone speak—someone you don't particularly like. You hear them make an inflammatory political statement that pretty much pisses you off.

It was actually the moment you decided that you don't like them that your brain began filtering information. Your brain stopped listening. Even worse, you heard an inflammatory statement. When that happened, your brain launched a full mental filter that further blocked you from listening. These filters are designed to focus only on the information that confirms your beliefs. Most everything else gets lost. What now? Brain-slap time. Suspend your beliefs for the sake of listening.

The best come prepared, meaning that it's worth the mental effort to work through your own biases about a person, or an idea, or a thing, before you hear them. Decide that you are going to suspend your beliefs. In the concepts of emotional self-management, we call this deconditioning a trigger. You know when you get triggered. Now know that whether you respond, shut down, or don't react, it is at least partly within your control.

INFLUENTIAL LISTENING

Unfortunately, all listening is not created equal. There's the type of listening that makes people want to work with you, the type that makes people hate you, and the spectrum in between. We are going to learn how to master the art of the right type of influential listening.

In everyday life, most people default to treating listening as an act of silence. However, why waste such an excellent opportunity to influence the speaker when it's your turn to speak? Listening with influence involves activating good body language and avoiding distractions.

Eye Contact, Facial Expressions, and "Stop Looking at Your Phone for One Damn Second"

Eye contact is an essential body language technique for listening because it both improves your ability to listen and signals to the speaker that they are important. By eye contact, I don't mean staring at the person the entire time, as that can get a bit creepy—but aim for at least 80 to 90 percent eye contact. That is, when someone is speaking, try to hold eye contact with them 80 to 90 percent of the time. You'll notice with practice that you become a far better listener through this simple trick alone.

As a person whose face shows my feelings, I'm pretty terrible at this skill. However, when it comes to good listening, your face must be inviting for the other person to want to speak, or the whole exercise becomes futile. Check in with your face when someone speaks. Feel for your face muscles and soften those muscles. Parting your teeth slightly is a common trick that yogis use to practice facial relaxation and create mental calm. In addition to improving your focus, this will help you act and look like a better listener. Whether you're nervous, scared, or downright pissed, keep your face soft and open (just like your brain, dear listener).

Perception is reality. The majority of us have an overconfidence bias when it comes to skills. We think we are above average drivers and that we can effectively multitask. Unfortunately, all the research shows that multitasking is a lie we tell ourselves. Put down your damn phone and keep it down until the end of the conversation. Show people you are committed to them and their message.

Wearable

I once saw a corporate executive smoothly check his smartwatch throughout a meeting without anyone else in the room even noticing. Wearable and other seamless technologies like them can assist you here if you have the type of job (or significant other) that requires your constant attention. Proceed at your own risk and be smooth about it.

FINDING MEANING IN THE MESSAGE

Finally, active listening is a search for meaning. Don't just listen to the words, seek to understand what the speaker truly means. Getting to the root cause of someone's words is where listening transforms into powerful communication. Listening involves dialogue, done correctly. Once someone has spoken, whether it's your boss, your social media followers, or a particularly unpleasant coworker, dive in.

Want to benefit further from listening? Research shows that when managers listen to employees for six hours per week, it boosts employee engagement by 30 percent, improves inspiration in employees' work by 29 percent, and boosts innovation by 16 percent. This means that implementing and practicing great listening skills in your business can boost emotional and financial gains from your workforce.

Ask Open Questions

According to a 2016 article published by Harvard Business Review, Harvard University researchers found that people who are perceived as excellent listeners had one significant difference in their approach: they ask a certain type of question. They ask questions that are open and designed to help the other person better understand the topic of the conversation. The more deeply you can understand the speaker, the easier it becomes to craft your communication to them. This can be done in a business meeting or even over Instagram. Keep the questions limited to ones that require a long response, not just a yes or no.

Avoid Leading Questions

Bad listeners were the ones who grabbed on to a piece of information and led it in a different direction. Remember to avoid this type of conversation hijacking. Focus on the topic while it's going. Listening is an act of patience.

Search for the Why behind the Words

Our primary goal as communicators is not to be the ones moving our mouths the most or using the fanciest words. It is to connect people to a message. To do this, we must know what they want and then craft our language to give them a version of it. That's what great communication does. Which is exactly why listening is the first communication skill we are reviewing. Sometimes people simply want to be heard. Other times, they want to persuade. But why is that? Seek out the why behind the person talking.

Ask and Ye Shall Receive

Ask open questions that build on the conversation. They can be as simple as, "Can you tell me more about _____?" or, "Can you give me an example?" or, "What led you to believe this?" Well-crafted open questions invite your speaker to dive deeper into the conversation. This will give you better listening skills and a better understanding of your listener and their message.

KEY CONCEPTS

- Clear your brain

- Listen for the purpose of actually listening and not responding

- Never cut off the speaker during a sentence

- Don't hijack a mentioned thought

- Stay on topic

- Maintain eye contact

- Practice Zen-like awareness of your facial expressions

- Listen free of technological distractions

- Ask open questions that seek deeper meaning

- Avoid leading questions

- Seek to understand your speaker

ASK YOURSELF

Listening is a key skill. In the next conversation you have, stop your mind from wandering or forming a sentence. Ask yourself: "Am I listening? Am I adding to the topic we're discussing? Am I maintaining eye contact and good body language? Am I not looking at my phone or getting distracted?" My friend and colleague, Cameron Herold, recently told me he sits on his hands when he's listening to remind himself to be an open listener. Whether you physically or mentally cue yourself in, check on your listening skills each time you communicate until it becomes second nature.

Chapter 3. Effective Communication Skills and Its Importance

Communication, quite simply, is defined as the exchanging of information that we do amongst ourselves and other individuals. This exchange of information can take place in the form of speaking, writing, signs, signals or behavior.

If you live in this world, you need to relate to others around you. Nobody can survive without having their needs met, and to have our needs met, whether we like it or not, requires the help of other individuals to do so. And therefore, we need to rely on communication to get by.

Communication is a skill that many don't think twice about, but it is one of the most important skills you could have at your disposal. If you want to know what it is like not to be able to communicate or be understood, just picture a time when you have gone to a foreign country where you do not speak the local language.

Everything suddenly becomes more difficult, doesn't it? You struggle to understand and to make yourself understood, and even simple forms of communication like asking for directions seems like an impossible task. Communication, both verbal and nonverbal, matters. It matters because it helps us relate and collaborate with the people living in the world with us.

There are several reasons why it is important to have effective communication skills in our everyday life, and those reasons include:

Effective Communication Helps Us Form Relationships

The foundation of all human relationships is how well you can bond with another person. Two people start off as strangers, and how do they form a bond from there? They start communicating. They interact, they start talking and start getting to know one another and slowly, a relationship begins to form, and it begins with being able to communicate effectively with one another.

Effective Communication Helps Express Ideas & Pass Information

Think of all the greatest inventions that we have in our lives today. All of those came to fruition because the inventors were able to communicate their brilliant ideas to the rest of the world. Effective communication is the reason people can facilitate the process of information and knowledge sharing so seamlessly. Without it, a lot of our ideas, thoughts, and points of view would just be trapped inside our heads, and we would not know what to do about it. If you can effectively master the art of communication and make it easy for people to understand, your chances of conveying the information without the danger of being completely misinterpreted will increase that much more.

Effective Communication Avoids Misunderstanding

We all know what happens when information is misunderstood or taken out of context. Heated arguments arise, fights happen, and sometimes relationships get severed because misunderstood information causes hurt feelings or hits a sore spot with someone. That is another major reason why effective communication is such a vital skill to possess. You exist in this world; you need to be able to express your messages clearly and to the point to minimize the chances that what you are going to say is going to cause problems for yourself and the people that you are speaking to.

Effective Communication Increases Your Confidence

Have you ever noticed how some of the most successful people in the world seem to ooze confidence? When they speak, the audience hangs onto their every word. That's because they're able to communicate well. When you can communicate effectively, your self-esteem and confidence level rise because you do not doubt at all that you can express and tell people exactly what you want them to know. When you can communicate well, you find that you are no longer shy and awkward when it comes time for you to speak, because you know exactly what to do and how to handle the situation.

Effective Communication Will Help You Go Far

Success cannot be achieved if you are not able to convey yourself properly. When people have a hard time understanding you, how will they be able to get along well with you? If you want to be successful at everything you do in life, you need to confidently be able to communicate effectively, because this is how you are going to set yourself apart from the rest. Do you notice how the most successful people in the world are the ones who can communicate effortlessly?

Mindset for Effective Communication

Before we begin our journey into critical conversations the first thing that we need to look at and master is our mindset. What most people don't know, realize or accept is that our mind is the

36

most underused and most understood organ in the human body. With our minds we can accomplish anything that we can possibly imagine as well as limit ourselves to the most basic of tasks and possibilities.

When it comes to mindset it all comes down to what it is that you want and what you are willing to do or not do to achieve it. When looking at mindset, look at it as a coin. On one side we have everything that we want and desire whereas on the other side of the coin we have all of the excuses and issues that prevent us from achieving our goals. For the majority of us however we walk the edge of the coin looking down at the shiny side of our hopes and desires while favoring or listening to the doubts and echoes from the other side.

This is where the conversation starts. What side of the coin are you going to choose?

Your Self Image

The next layer of our mindset can be found in our self-image. The way that we look at ourselves and the way we perceive others looking at us is a major factor in our mindset and the actions that we engage. For instance, if you are someone who is overweight, doesn't speak well, has a disability or just doesn't feel right physically or emotionally your self-image will be affected by this. One the other side of the coin if you are slender, well educated, has a lot of friends and is healthier than ever your self-image will be greater resulting in more positive outcomes and conversations.

Knowing your abilities and limitations

The third level of mindset is our personal knowledge and understanding of our abilities and limitations. To start this off I want to first say that no one is perfect. If you believe you are perfect, then you are living in a delusional world and are going to be in for a huge disappointment in life. However, if you know that you are not perfect and can accept that you have limitations then you have the foundation to build form and grow.

When we know and accept our limitations, we can better position ourselves into situations that we feel comfortable and in control. If we feel comfortable and in control, we are more likely to be in a better frame of mind to have more intelligent conversations with our inner voices. If, however, we find ourselves in situations that we are not comfortable in it is our job to restructure our mindsets to work in a positive way. And we can do this with critical conversations.

You are an island among many

The final component in regard to mindset is one that is seldom talked about or referred to. This is the knowledge that you are an island among many. What this basically means is that you are responsible for you first and foremost. Where many of us fall into the mindset trap is that we think of others first instead of ourselves. Now, I am not saying that you need to be selfish and self-centered. What I am saying is that at the end of the day when all of the kids are asleep, you are lying there in bed wide awake staring at the ceiling letting the events of the day fill your mind just know that you are one with yourself.

The actions that you perform or fail to perform will ultimately affect you in the end. Your kids will one day go off to school, your spouse may divorce you, you may lose or find another job, get a new house, car or win the lottery or eventually die. It is when we find ourselves in these situations, we really begin to have these critical conversations with ourselves. Knowing how we plan to handle these conversations when they arrive will ultimately determine their outcomes.

Developing Assertiveness in Communication

One of the most vital skills to be an effective leader and communicator is developing assertiveness, which is starkly different from aggression. Assertiveness is standing up for yourself and not focusing on pleasing everyone all the time. This is done in a manner that is polite, firm, and non-offensive to others. Assertiveness is taking a balanced, reasonable, and win-win approach that considers the overall good. For instance, "I prefer going to a relaxed coffee shop rather than fine-dine restaurant" is a fairly assertive statement. It doesn't pronounce a judgment about what you want. It gives the other person an opportunity to give his/her view about it too. You are mentioning your preferences in a rational and balanced manner.

Assertiveness is clarifying your needs without using aggression or dominance. While aggressiveness involves disregard for another person's rights or needs, assertiveness is about putting across your needs in a polite, firm, and respectful manner. Unlike aggression that focuses on 'I win-you lose', assertiveness is about win-win. Take the aggressive version of the above-mentioned assertive statement. "We are going nowhere else but a relaxed cafe." This doesn't leave any scope for the other person to offer their views.

Assertive folks may not agree with a person. However, they will still respect the person's right to his opinion, beliefs, ideas, and preferences. They often respect the person's right to disagree. "We can agree to disagree" is a classic assertive statement. You don't give up your stand, and also respect the other person's right to stick to their stand. As an assertive person, you don't allow people to walk over you and know where to draw the line, while also respecting other people's values. Mutual respect and equality are the buzzwords of assertiveness.

Here are a few strategies to be a more assertive communicator:

One secret tip for building greater assertiveness is practicing in front of a mirror. Pretend that your boss, employee, team member, partner, or friend is standing opposite you. Have a mock interaction with them, where there are getting you to do something you don't to do. How best can you communicate this in an open, polite, firm, genuine, and non-offensive manner? Concentrate on everything from your expressions to words to body language. Watch out for the tone of your voice. How do you emphasize certain words to sound more assertive? When do you pause to create the right effect of what you've just said?

Practicing this for a while will help you convey your point in a polite and balanced way.

Use more than "I" statements to accept responsibility for your emotions, thoughts, ideas, and feeling. For instance, instead of "we should never go to that restaurant" say, "I think we should avoid going to that restaurant." It prevents you from appearing dictatorial or dogmatic. Again, if you feel upset about your partner not contributing towards the baby's care, you can say something like, "I feel really upset that I wake up several times in the night. I need your help in caring for the baby."

Always view other people as a force you are working or collaborating with instead of working against them. This is even truer in work settings. Some people are always operating with the mentality that someone has to lose if they have to win. This isn't a sign of assertiveness.

Chapter 4. Effective Oral Communication

The 7%-38%-55% Rule

In communication, a speaker's words are just a small amount of his endeavors. The tone, speed, and mood of his verbally expressed words, and the pauses between those words may express more than what is being conveyed by words alone. Further, his motions, stance, posture, and articulations more often than not pass on an assortment of different signs. These non-verbal characteristics can give an audience significant hints on information regarding the speaker's musings and sentiments and, in this way, prove the truth of the speaker's words.

The most normally cited study on this matter is one by Albert Mehrabian, Professor Emeritus of Psychology at the University of California, Los Angeles. During the 1970s, his examinations proposed that we overwhelmingly tend to reason our emotions, frames of mind, and convictions about what somebody says not by the genuine words verbally expressed, but by the speaker's non-verbal communication and manner of speaking.

The truth, Prof. Mehrabian evaluated this inclination: words, manner of speaking, and non-verbal communication separately represent 7%, 38%, and 55% of individual communication.

As a matter of fact, when a speaker's words together with their non-verbal communication contrast, audience members are bound to accept the nonverbal communication of the speaker, not his words. For instance, if an individual states, "I don't have an issue with you!" while evading eye to eye connection, looking restless, and keeping up a shut non-verbal communication, the audience will likely confide in the predominant type of communication, which as per Prof. Mehrabian's discoveries is non-verbal (38% + 55%), as opposed to the strict significance of the words (7%.)

In my opinion, there are two possible objections that can counter an overly simplistic interpretation of "Rule 7-38-55". First of all, it is not easy to understand how much the paraverbal and non-verbal language on the effectiveness of communication counts. And then, these quantifications are very subjective and cannot be applied universally to any context. The same Prof. Mehrabian has warned us about this.

Non-verbal components are especially significant for communicating emotions and frame of mind, particularly when they are incongruent: if words and non-verbal communication differ, one will, in general, accept the non-verbal communication.

Indicated by Mehrabian, the three components account diversely for our preference for the individual who advances a message concerning their sentiments: words represent 7%, manner of speaking records for 38%, and non-verbal communication represents 55% of the enjoying.

When talking about powerful and significant communication about feelings, these three pieces of the message need to help one another - they must be "consistent." If there should arise an occurrence of any incongruence, the beneficiary of the message may be disturbed by two messages originating from two unique channels, giving prompts in two distinct ways.

The accompanying model should help show inconsistencies in verbal and non-verbal communication. "I don't have an issue with you!" The individual keeps away from eye to eye connection, looks on edge has a shut non-verbal connection, and so on.

It turns out to be more probable that the beneficiary will confide in the dominating type of communication, which to Mehrabian's discoveries is the non-verbal effect of tone and gestures (38% + 55%), as opposed to the exact importance of the words (7%). This is known as "the 7%-38%-55% Rule".

It is imperative to state that in a separate investigation, Mehrabian led examinations managing communications of emotions and frames of mind (i.e., like-hate) and that the above mentioned, lopsided impact of the manner of speaking and non-verbal communication winds up convincing just when the circumstance is vague. Such vagueness shows up for the most part when the words verbally expressed are conflicting with the manner of speaking or non-verbal communication of the speaker (sender).

The "7%-38%-55% principle" has been generally misjudged. It is frequently guaranteed in any communication that the significance of the information is passed on mostly by the use of non-verbal prompts and not through the importance of words. The speculation from the - at first unmistakable states in his analyses is the normal misstep made in connection to Mehrabian's standard.

This examination is a helpful—if not exact—update that nonverbal prompts can be more important and telling than verbal ones. Along these lines, to be viable and convincing in our verbal communication — in introductions, open talking, or individual communication — it is basic to supplement our words with the correct tone and voice and the fitting non-verbal communication.

Communication Styles

The work by Dr. Eileen Russo is shown beneath. It demonstrates that two distinct measurements in communication styles are present: the degree of how to express oneself and the degree of emphatics.

Every image speaks to an alternate communication style. Individuals can fall anyplace inside every quadrant, fusing up consistently more than one particular style over the others further from the mid-point. Take note that more emphatic communication styles tend to dictate to others what to do. While the less decisive communication styles tend to request of others what ought to be finished.

The most expressive communication styles will, in general, demonstrate their feelings outwardly, discourse, and tone. The less expressive kind will choose to either not express their feelings or work on them. Below you can find the four fundamental communication styles. In the accompanying segments, we'll take a gander at the fundamental attributes of every communication style and a few things you can do to help your communication well with each sort.

Spirited Communication Style

The spirited communication style is keen on a 'master plan.' Those who use this style are the visionaries, the creators, and the pioneers in the gathering. Their communication might be brimming with fantastic thoughts and exaggerations that will, in general, be influential to others from the start.

They are not, in every case, truly adept at talking about subtleties and tend to make stories seem more fantastic then they may seem. It is common for people who are spirited communicators to go off on tangents.

Their composed verbal communication may tend to sound more sensational. While they can be exceptionally engaging, getting them to convey plainly on specific points may take the help of another person to direct them through a discussion and keep them on track by taking them back to the current subject.

Tips on how to relate and communicate if you use a spirited style:

- When thinking about new plans to share, likewise think about whether you have recommendations on the most proficient method to place those thoughts into activity.

- Respect settled upon plans that have been set to run meetings.

- Try to restrict sharing individual stories that will sway off the subject of the discussion.

- Be sure to enable others to share their thoughts and recommendations while at the same time, you are tuning in.

- Be sure any solicitations you make are clear, and any inquiries are open to being made.

- Share your gratefulness for other individuals who have put forth work and effort.

Tips on how to relate with individuals with the spirited communication style:

- Use motivation with time breaking points recorded for every subject.

- Praise them before other individuals.

- Learn to divert the discussion back to the current subject delicately.

- Understand that they may misrepresent.

50

- Challenge them to separate their' huge thoughts' into precise results and steps.

- Agree to assist where you can in what they are willing to partake in.

- Use registration or other composed updates as a way to help convey what should be finished.

Examples of Spirited Communication Style:

When speaking with somebody who is spirited, it may be challenging to try and keep them on the subject at hand. What's more, when you have their attention, keeping it is another issue entirely. You will find that consistency is essential while speaking with spirited individuals. If you can get them used to a specific arrangement or strategy for communication, it will be simpler to keep them focused and engaged. This doesn't mean continually picking email over choosing the phone just because it is their preference. However, it means regularly utilizing follow-up inquiries or monitoring a standard premise to check whether you are both still in agreement.

Here's a case of a decently composed communication to a spirited individual.

'Hello there, Sally!

I thought your introduction yesterday was awesome! I delighted in the manner that you had the group of spectators take part in the session.

I figure you would be an extraordinary decision for the instructive segment at our next executive gathering. The Board of Directors needs some data about nearby financial patterns, however, in a way that isn't too exhausting or convoluted.

Would you prefer to talk about this over lunch? I'm free on Thursday or Friday this week. Fill me in regarding whether both of those days will work for you.

Much appreciated!

George'

For what reason would this communication work for a spirited individual? It is energetic, integral, and would complement Sally. She will be satisfied that you saw her first introduction and increasingly confident that you might want her to rehash it.

Of course, you're sure to have an exceptionally energized individual on your hands at lunch. So be ready. You could bring a diagram of the points you need to cover in the introduction. Request her info and ensure you've arranged sufficient opportunities to let her give it. At that point, help her lay the thoughts down and note them for her. Sending a subsequent email or note will help guarantee that you are both on a similar page also.

Keep in mind, the spirited individual is valuable for every one of their abilities and every bit of excitement, so with a little structure around your interactions, you can be successful in communicating without smothering the very characteristics they bring to the table.

Direct Communication Style

As demonstrated in the communication style grid, individuals with a direct communication style are profoundly decisive and not expressive. They will, in general, instruct others as opposed to asking others what they think ought to be done, and they won't effortlessly indicate feelings in their communications with others. Their communication style is intended to be practical. However, others may not always see it that way. They may seem brisk and cold to other people, who may think about their style of communicating literally.

This style will let others know exactly how they feel before proceeding onward to the following subject, not because they are attempting to be shifty, but because they are trying to spare time. They won't generally stop to tune in to other people, regardless of whether the others have something significant to contribute. They may appear to be restless and domineering now and again, yet it's not intended to be received that way.

They are trying to concentrate on results as opposed to feelings. They will express their real thoughts, regardless of whether it could be off-putting to other people. Try not to anticipate that they will discuss their own lives—they like to keep business and individual issues isolated. They don't give up and on occasion, could be viewed as being forceful as opposed to decisive due to the manner that they express their assessments.

Tips on how to communicate while having a direct communication style:

- Always listen completely to other people and abstain from hindering.

- Create time for 'talking' toward the start of a gathering.

- Allow others to express their feelings about points.

Recognize that conceptualizing can be useful and not only a 'period squanderer.'

Chapter 5. Main and Common Obstacles for Having Effective Communication

Get to Know Your Obstacles!

A good idea is to ask the people you see most about what you should improve in yourself (or even change totally) when it comes to your way of communicating. It might appear like a strange idea at first, but believe me, it's one of the most effective ways of inner transformation. Your friends, family or coworkers (interlocutors in general) may often see some aspects of your communication (sometimes as subtle as tone of voice, facial expression, etc.) that you are completely unaware of. Now, let me tell you about the most common obstacles on your way to becoming an effective communicator. Take a moment to reflect on each of these points very deeply and honestly. No need to deceive yourself. Answer yourself: are you doing these things often?

Playing a Judge

Perhaps you are certain that your way of perceiving the world is the only correct way? If you tend to show judging behaviors, you may have a tendency to interpret your interlocutor's messages through mental filters of stereotypes or your own beliefs and experiences. Feeling like you are the only one with the right to be right will turn out to be wrong and unfair.

Feeling the Need to Finish the Words of Other People

It is very frustrating for people around you and can make them unwilling to continue the conversation, even if you are not told directly. In some instances, if it happens constantly, it can even contribute to the ending of your relationships because a listener does not try to analyze what a sender is trying to say. If you are a frequent interrupter, do everything you can to stop this tendency. You could, for example, imagine yourself as a journalist conducting an interview with a VIP, in serious need to gain as much information as possible about the other person.

Uncle Good Advice

When you share your observations and give others advice, you almost always feel like you can surely help them or contribute to solving their problems. Step back and take a moment to think about how you feel when other people are constantly giving you their advice (especially unwanted advice). How does it make you feel? Instead of playing a good uncle and giving your "helpful tips" to everyone ("If I were you, I would…"), try putting yourself in your interlocutor's place or situation and reflecting on how you would feel when something like that happened to you. Eventually, you can give advice if that's your field of expertise or you're asked for it. Only just enough advice and not too much, only an honest attempt to understand your interlocutor deeply and nothing more.

Moralizer

Similar to "Uncle Good Advice," but even worse as it's totally pointless. Does your style of conversation have features of a moralizer? "Every intelligent man put in your place…" "You can't just say that to people!" "Who do you think you are?" "How can you listen to this kind of nasty music?" "How can you wear these bright colored clothes all the time? If I were you…" "When I was your age I never…!" Are these the sentences that you say often? If the answer is yes, really think about what you want to achieve by saying these things. Try to avoid that kind of sentence as often as possible, unless you want to be perceived as a hunchbacked grumpy old aunt with a never-ending headache, chronic back pain and a fiery hatred for cute, small animals.

Being "The Talker"

Maybe you have a tendency for too many frequent, excessive utterances, meaning that your mouth rarely shuts. On one hand, it can be a feature of your openness, knowledge or high intelligence. On the other hand, such need for a constant self-expression can be overwhelming for others.

This feature is rarely required in everyday situations (only sometimes, when you first meet someone, when they're shy and you want to kick start the talk) and makes it difficult to receive genuine info about other people (and also feedback about yourself) during the conversation. It feels like hanging out with a parrot or an actor rehearsing his annoying monologue for the fiftieth time before a big play. This was my big obstacle and the reason I was able to date many nice girls back in my high school days, but without a chance for a second or third meeting. I simply talked way too much and rarely listened to them and it took me many wrecked first impressions and sleepless nights to figure that out. They probably felt like they were having dinner or a walk with a TV screen. Many men have problems with that.

Even today I can talk A LOT and once I start firing words, I often have to force myself to stop, thinking, and "Easy, you will have time to say all these things, but not yet. You are not here alone! Chill out, dude."

People Who Don't Let You Speak

Opposite to above, you may have a tendency for submission in relationships with others. Do you have the impression that others are not interested in your opinion? Do you often find yourself in situations where your interlocutor takes advantage of your attention and does not let you speak? Think about the reason beneath such situations.

Maybe you have a bad opinion about yourself ("I have nothing interesting to say"). Maybe you are afraid of other people's reactions when you want to interrupt a conversation or simply add to it. Do not let that happen. You have the same right to speak as others have. If you feel bad during a conversation (someone is overwhelming you by their talking), just stop them, politely tell them about it or try to change the subject. Don't waste your time and energy.

The key phrase is, "So, you're telling me…" It's a great navigational tool to use in conversations with people who tend to often jump from one topic to another and talk about one hundred different things in a matter of a few minutes. I have this business partner who tends to lose track often in his conversations. He really is a big talker. If you took him to a business meeting and asked him to quickly tell you how he got into the retail business and what his background was, he would tell you something like: "Well, that's an interesting question. In 1979, I was a military school dropout. Before that, I originally wanted to become a pilot because I always wanted to be paid for playing with grown-man toys, and you know, the military planes are so fascinating. I don't know if you've heard about the new project for US army stealth-planes, but they can fly above the stratosphere and they're equipped with the newest…" and then he would tell you everything he knows about military, soldiers, their families, their friends and dogs. He would probably love to tell you a story longer than all nine seasons of How I Met Your Mother put together.

What you need to do to politely interrupt in that situation is to take any of the last sentences that person said and repeat it back, prefacing it with, "So, you're telling me." So if my friend got to that point, I would tell him something like: "So, you're telling me that these new planes can fly really high, right?"

And normally when you say something like that to people, they respond by saying, "Yes, I was telling you that…but why did you ask me?" and then they go back right on the track. "Ah yes, I'm a mechanical engineer." Or if they forget the original question, you just need to repeat it and they get right to the answer you wanted to hear, but they are not offended that you are interrupted them, because you interrupted them while showing that you are listening to them carefully at the same time. As an effective communicator, you will sometimes have to lead the conversation where it needs to go.

Comforting Words

There is nothing wrong with comforting someone, at least at first glance. When we comfort someone, we have good intentions. We want to show that a certain situation isn't as bad as they might think, and it will get better. But clichés like: "Don't worry, there will be a new day tomorrow," "Others may be in a worse situation than you are," or a very common saying, "Keep your head up!" usually bring exactly the opposite effect. These sentences usually show a low level of communication abilities. Remove them from your list of usual reactions. What you can do instead is this simple process: That might be, for example: "Really? That's what people expect to hear rather than, "It's not bad," or, "Don't worry," which would mean they are exaggerating, overreacting or creating an artificial problem.

Losing Focus

Perhaps it is also difficult for you to stay concentrated or focus on something for longer periods of time? Maybe you often show your impatience non-verbally. If that's the case, you should dedicate a good bit of time to improving your focus.

By mastering the ability of concentration on what other people say to you, you get more valuable information. This enables you to focus on the real benefits of connecting with others and also allows you to be there, in the moment, which not only makes you much more likeable, but also more effective as a communicator.

Let's now quickly recap what you just learned about basic communication obstacles. To communicate effectively and avoid distraction tendencies mentioned above, you have to remember some basic rules:

1.   Do not judge others; try to separate your own interpretations from what your interlocutor really said.

2.   Listen patiently to the entire conversation and paraphrase often—the latter makes you rehearse what you have just been told and keeps your mind from wandering away. Not only that, but it also creates a very good impression of a genuine listener.

3.   Instead of handing out advice all the time, pay attention and show readiness to find something interesting in your conversation.

4.   Give people you talk to a chance to show their beliefs, even if they are quite different from yours. Do not show disapproval in the form of moralizing, such as "Not bad, but when I was your age…," or, "But I would do it differently and more efficiently," etc.

5.   Try to notice your interlocutor's subtle emotional reactions (you have to actually look at them when you talk) to know if your utterances are overly expanded or not.

6.   Remember that you have the same right to express yourself as everyone else. If you feel overwhelmed, don't stop yourself from telling people who talk too much that you disapprove of this.

7.   Instead of comforting with cheesy clichés, just learn to show interest and approval to your interlocutor.

8. Work on your concentration (e.g. by applying regular meditation and relaxation techniques), and endeavor to understand other people's real intentions.

9. If possible, communicate face to face. Nowadays, we have a plague of Facebook and e-mail quarrels, serious arguments and even break-ups. When you don't see who you're talking to, you can't recognize their emotions. Written communication is also often dishonest: people accuse somebody of something or offend them and read the answer whenever they want to (or never), not giving the other person a chance for a direct reaction. Poor and weak…but unfortunately more and more common. It's so easy to hide beneath your computer screen, but it's hard to say these things face to face.

Chapter 6. Emphatic Communication

It can be best described as a way to pass or receive information while considering one's actions. It includes taking into account a person's steps, how they perform the steps, why they perform the activities, and the effect the steps have on other people. This type of self-awareness makes it easier for people to communicate and connect with other people. For any kind of relationship, emphatic communication is paramount, because it will enable the people in the partnership to identify with the feelings of the other person and communicate in a way that does not affect them negatively.

Emphatic communication makes it easier for one to express their feelings, ideas, and have a better chance of correctly responding to other people. It is an important skill to have, because it improves a person's ability to perform, at the same time enhancing other people's ability to function. Thus, it increases efficiency, friendliness, and effectiveness.

Enacting Emphatic Listening in a Relationship

Ask Questions

To start a conversation, it is best to start by asking questions. The type of questions that are proposed as a conversation opener has to be neutral. This means that sensitive topics such as religion, politics, and gender have to be steered clear of. Asking questions ensures that a person considers the feelings of the other person first, and quickly learns their opinion on topics that are not as neutral.

Avoid Judgments

Every person on earth has a bias, and this is especially true when it comes to sensitive topics. Thus, to enact emphatic communication, one should avoid judging. One should listen keenly, and refrain from judging the other person at all cost. The other person in the relationship should feel like they are being listened to, and their point of view is being understood. Simply put, when communicating with someone, the listener should be able to walk a mile in the other person's shoes, and understand their point of view. In case there are arguments, they should be presented in a manner that is not judgmental.

Pay Attention

There is nothing as unnerving as talking to someone who is not actively paying attention to the communication process. It makes a person lose interest and not open up as much as they want to. Thus, secure communication should be achieved by paying attention to the person speaking, be it in a group or a private setting. Distractions such as noise, phones, and other gadgets should be done away with, and the speaker is given undivided attention. It will enable the listener to identify the feelings of the speaker by reading the body language and respond accordingly.

Refrain From Giving Unsolicited Advice

A popular pitfall to emphatic communication is giving advice or sharing one's point of view, even when the speaker has not sought it. At times, all a person wants is to be listened to. Giving advice that has not been asked for impedes this process, and the person will not be able to communicate their feelings effectively.

Thus, for empathic communication to occur, refrain from giving advice, unless the speaker directly asks for it. Additionally, sharing one's opinion on a subject is good.

However, it communicates to the speaker is that the listener is self-centered and does not consider the feelings of other people. At times, giving advice can generate resistance from the other party, and they stop communicating what they wanted to pass on. Thus, the objective of the conversation should be kept in mind at all times during the communication process.

Use the LSF Method

The LSF method is a synonym for Listening-Summarizing-Follow up. It is a popular method used for achieving emphatic listening.

Listening involves actively paying attention to what someone is saying and being in the moment. Active listening involves someone reading body language, the environment, and focusing on the matter in the message. It also means that the listener should be devoid of any distractions and encourage the other person to open up more by using encouraging words, and asking questions when necessary. It is the first step of the technique because it is how the message is passed on.

Summarizing can either be done verbally or non-verbally. When done verbally, it can be a discussion with the speaker to clarify if what was understood, what was intended to be passed along.

Summarization can also be done in one's mind, as the communication process ensues. It indicates that the listener has understood what has been said, the way it was intended. Keywords have to be used during the summarization process so that the listener can know that the main message was passed along. Depending on the situation, it is better to summarize verbally, so that any clarifications can be made.

Follow-up is whereby connections are made in the information given. For instance, a person can start a conversation by talking about one thing, and then link it up with something else. Follow up allows the listener to get clarification on how the linkages occur, and if what has been understood was what was meant to be communicated. It can also be to make connections with other things that are not part of the conversation. During follow up, it is essential to make sure that the goal of the communication process is kept in mind.

When using this method to enact emphatic communication, it is paramount that a person's emotions are considered, and acknowledged loudly. It makes the speaker see that the listener can relate or understands their point of view. Thus, a speaker can say, "I see this upsets you" to the listener when he says something that is upsetting to them.

Silence

Silence is powerful, especially in a conversation. It makes sure the listener can take in what has been said, and digest it, and give time for summarization. It helps the listener understand what the other person is trying to say and give room for the other person to organize their thoughts.

Short bouts of silence can be used to enact emphatic communication because they are a way for the listener to understand what the speaker is saying. It also gives room to a person to do away with their biases, and get the point from the other person's point of view, according to their background. Thus, silence during a conversation should not be seen as awkward, but a practical way to ensure empathic communication.

Managing short instances of silence is a skill that takes time to master. Thus, the listener should practice it so that they do not become awkward or indicate the end of the conversation.

Raise Attention Levels by Self-Detachment and Decreasing Self-Centralization

Seeing a point from someone else's point of view or experience is hard, and has to be learned. Thus, to increase attention, one has to detach themselves from their experiences and biases, and pay attention to the other person. It helps a person be in the moment, and solely understand what is being said at the moment.

Self-centeredness is an inherent human trait because it helps people survive. It helps people identify what is right for them and assist in the decision-making process. However, it can impede empathic communication because one will be blind from the other person's reality. Therefore, self-decentralization should occur, and the existence of the other interculotor should be more critical. It is the only way that emphatic communication can occur.

Self-detachment and decentralization increase attention levels, when listening, one will not be making connections to the information given to their own lives. Instead, the listener will understand the information provided, free of bias or judgment.

Read the Speaker

People might communicate one thing and mean the other. It happens to the nest of us, especially when we are nervous, or afraid of judgment. However, body language does not lie and will always betray what the speaker wants to say. This is why the listener should read the speaker.

A listener should be keen on the emotions that are behind what is being said. It will help in the emphatic communication process because the listener will be able to relate to the feelings that the speaker has. It will also help when giving responses, as the speaker will understand how to provide the answers.

Reading the body language also helps one understand the information that is being left out. Some information is tough to let out, but one might let out snippets of it. It is up to the listener to read between the lines and assure the speaker that he understands what is trying to be communicated.

This skill helps in the dynamic communication process because it puts one in the shoe of the speaker. It improves the effectiveness and connections made during the communication process. The speaker is more likely to open up when they are always reassured that their message is reaching home.

Take Action

Emphatic communication is meeting the needs of the other person. Thus, after being communicated to, one should take action and meet the other person at the point of their needs. It does not have to be the right action, but any activity that would help them overcome their situation.

A person might communicate that they do not seem to get a hold of their finances. An action that can be taken is teaching them simple methods of saving, referring them to someone who can help them. The most important part is their opinion has to be sort on which option is the best and let them make that decision for themselves.

In a relationship, empathy should not only be practiced when there is a crisis. It should be something that should be done at all times. Therefore, in every conversation held, one should be able to see the point from the other person's point of view, in any situation. Judgments should not be commonplace, and one should strive to widen their perspective on many issues.

Actions help build emphatic communication because they communicate that a person is reliable, and the listener is likely to communicate the next time they have an issue.

Understand That Perception is everything

Psychology states that empathy involves communication and perception. Communication can occur at any time, but perception is very important, especially when one wants to build an emphatic connection.

People often understand what they want to, depending on their experiences and background. Thus, what is being communicated might not be what will be understood. Stephen Covey once said that "Many do not even listen with the intent to understand; they listen with the intent to reply." Ideally, many people are either speaking or are listening with the intent to reply. Therefore, conversations are like monologues because they are from one person's point of view.

Perception is everything because it develops emphatic communication. It enables a person to understand what is going on inside another human being, and this helps any action taken henceforth to be from another person's point of view. It also ensures productive conversations take place because it will be from the point of view of each person involved.

Perception also prevents conflict because of the understanding that needs to take place in the course of the conversation. Thus, to ensure empathic communication, one should make perception of their priority, and understand that there is always more to what is seen or being said.

Connect with the Environment

Everyone needs to learn, and also has something to teach others. Thus, a person should make it their goal to connect with people in the background. It broadens a person's point of view and develops their ability to see life from different perspectives. Being closed in is a limitation, and dramatically impedes a person's communication skills.

Chapter 7. Small Talk for Big Rapport Building

Now that we've tackled active listening, let us move on to another effective communication and rapport-building secret—small talk. Small talk can, indeed, create big magic when it comes to wowing people and building lasting relationships. There is something about people who have mastered small talk. They are charming, irresistible, and possessing of the knack of sweeping people off their feet instantly. This magnetism and charisma help them climb dizzy heights of popularity. Have you ever noticed how some people almost always manage to be crowd-pullers at every party or event? These are the glib talkers who make people feel comfortable and engrossed in a conversation.

All of us know someone who slays it when it comes to connecting with others or building a favorable rapport. The person knows precisely what to say and how to say it for creating the desired effect. How do they manage to capture people's attention every single time? Small talk or making conversation is not an inborn trait. It is something the person has mastered over a period of time, and you can do so as well!

They make it seem effortless and smooth. It seems like these savvy conversationalists can never say anything wrong.

What is this secret for being an incredible people magnet that small talk experts have mastered, and others do not know? Trust me—there's no magic wand or genie involved. There are high chances these people have painstakingly studied and conquered the art of building a rapport with others through the power of small talk. Small talk can be huge when it comes to building a favorable rapport with people and connecting at a deeper or more subconscious level.

A study has revealed that when we meet someone for the first time, it takes the person only 4 seconds to build an impression about us, which largely stays the same throughout our future interactions with them. Think about it—you have only 4 seconds to make a positive impression on people. Sounds scary? The idea is to give people a sense of belongingness and affiliation to make them feel comfortable in your company and to make the first interaction memorable.

Studies at Michigan University have demonstrated that small talk and thoughtful interactions increase our problem-solving mechanisms. Constructive and meaningful communication comprises getting a hold of other people's thoughts and trying to look at things from their perspective. This is vital when it comes to considering a problem from different angles and coming to a solution. It helps people develop strategic thinking, problem-solving skills, and lateral thinking.

Did you think about why some people are almost always successful when it comes to making friends, grabbing complimentary drinks at the bar, making unforgettable conversation, and generally sweeping others off their feet? The answer, in simple words, is small talk. It is indeed critical when it comes to making a favorable first impression, and getting them interested in interacting with you more often.

Yes, small talk seems like a mammoth task to some people. They break into a sweat when it comes to approaching strangers or initiating a conversation with unknown people. The ice-breaking gives them jitters, and they believe they will make a complete fool of themselves. The fact remains that you don't have much time to create a first impression, and whatever you say or do can break or make that crucial initial interaction. Small talk is indeed the foundation of every fulfilling and rewarding personal, social, and professional association. We form mutually rewarding and beneficial relationships on the basis of a favorable first impression or connection establishing small talk.

The objective of small talk is to show the other person how interesting, well-informed, and credible you are as an individual. It is also related to rapport building—creating a common ground to feel a sense of oneness or belongingness with the other person and for supporting future interactions.

By engaging in small talk, you can successfully determine if the people are indeed worthy of associating with you in the future for building more meaningful, rewarding, and beneficial social, professional, and personal associations. At times, causal talks can lead to lasting relationships with folks who are similar to you or in a similar situation as you.

Bedazzle people by building a positive first impression using these incredibly helpful small talk rules:

1. Always Stick to Safe, Neutral, and Non-Controversial Topics

When you are talking to someone for the first time or initial few times, as a thumb rule, go with more neural, evergreen, and universal topics. Don't pick culturally, religiously, and politically sensitive topics where people can have diverse views. This is even truer when you are talking to people from diverse nationalities, cultures, races, and so on. What are some safe and evergreen topics? Environment, movies, local city, health, and medical research, technology, weather, books, science, and so on. Avoid talking about war, political ideologies, religious differences, terrorism, and global conflicts.

Try to figure out your common ground and stick to it throughout the conversation. For example, if you realize that the person you are interacting with is an avid foodie, go with topics such as new eateries in town, popular city regional foods, international delicacies, and other similar food-related topics. Then again, if you realize that someone is a big sports fan, talk about weekend games, best places for games buffs to go to within and around town and winning game strategies. I am willing to bet my last cent people will be all charged to make an enthusiastic, spirited, and engaging conversation.

Many luxury vehicle salespersons are actually trained to identify their potential customer's interest so that they can build upon it to strike a favorable rapport. For example, if they come across gym equipment or gear in the vehicle, the salespeople will start talking about their cardio training sessions or weight training routine. They will offer muscle building tips or discuss healthy eating. The aim of this strategy is to boost the salesperson's likeability, build a positive rapport, leave behind a stellar first impression on the prospective customer, which boosts their chances of selling to the potential customer.

2. Look at the Day's News before Attending a Party or Networking Event

This is one of the best tips when it comes to conquering small talk like a boss. Before attending an important gathering, networking event, or party, stay abreast of the day's latest news, events, and happenings. It helps to stay well-informed and up to date with what is happening around you while making small talk. This makes you come across as an intelligent, interesting, and articulate person. Just before you head towards the vent, dedicate a few minutes for browsing through the day's important news stories. Use this for creating a "conversation starter bank." You have all the matter you need to initiate an engaging conversation instead of being at a loss of words or not knowing where to begin. You can simply start with any one of the ready topics and open the door for an interesting, meaningful, and memorable conversation.

Ensure that you do not go after controversial topics related to politics, international conflict, and debatable global affairs. Instead opt for relatively safe subjects such as a breakthrough in medical or technological research, new scientific trends, and so on, where there is little scope for a difference in opinion. You don't want to start World War 3 in a ballroom, do you? When you keep a conversation bank ready, it ensures that there aren't a lot of awkward minutes of silence or pointless fillers. This helps you keep other people completely hooked to the talk!

3. Mirroring

If there is one powerful tip that has existed since primordial times for building rapport and feeling a sense of oneness with a person, it is mirroring. It is the key that helps us establish a positive rapport with other people at a subconscious level. Mirroring has been in place throughout evolution and is still one of the best ways to get people to like you or feel that you are 'one among them.' The human brain is wired to identify people who are similar to them. We are invariably drawn or attracted to people who appear to be similar to us. There is an instant connection with people who are similar to us or like us at a highly subconscious level.

The best way to make a person feel that you are similar to at a deeper, subconscious level without them even noticing it is to simply mirror their actions, words, gestures, and so on. If you are on a mission to build a favorable impression on someone you have just met, mirror their actions, gestures, movements, voice, choice of words, and posture. Carefully notice their non-verbal and verbal signals, and mirror it for creating a sense of belongingness, likeability, and familiarity.

An expert tip is to keep your mirroring actions subtle and discreet to avoid giving the other person the impression that you are mimicking them. Use this technique for leading people to think that you are just 'one among them' or like them. This not just increases your likeability factor but also helps build a favorable rapport with anyone.

All you have to do is smartly identify the most words or phrases used by the person and drop them subtly while talking to them. For instance, if you find someone calling their business as their "empire," use the same word when you refer to their business. What happens when you do this? On a highly subconscious level, this increases your chances of getting the person to not just like you or feel a sense of oneness with you but also relate to you on a deeper plane, thus leading to a glowing first impression.

Bear in mind that the mirroring should look natural, subtle, and effortless. It shouldn't appear forced or like you ate trying to make a huge effort to get into someone's good books. Avoid looking nervous about identifying and aping every action or gesture the person makes. This will defeat the entire purpose of this strategy. This not just boosts your appeal but also facilitates the process of helping people bond with you more efficiently. People will respond and relate to you more favorably when you pitch yourself as a person who they are able to identify with.

4. Disagree in a Respectful and Matured Manner

While making small talk, you may not agree with everything the other person says. However, learn to disagree in a healthy, balanced, and respectful manner without getting offensive, aggressive, and confrontational. This will damage your chances of creating a positive impression on the other person. Use a more diplomatic and genuine approach such as, "This is a novel, different, and interesting way of looking at it or considering things. I never thought about it this way. Can you elaborate?" Now, this approach will keep things pleasant, while still showing disagreement. A potentially volatile situation can quickly turn into one of the constructive and healthy discussions. Learn to spot potentially negative conversations and quickly change them into pleasant interactions by using a more balanced approach, where you can make your point without offending the other person. Being assertive without coming across as aggressive in your interactions is the key to being an ultra-effective communicator. Aggression is, "I am always right, and you are always wrong," while assertiveness is, "I have the right to be my view, and so do you. Let us agree to disagree without changing our views."

Chapter 8. Empathy: A Winning Tool to Communicate

People are more familiar with the word "sympathy", which means to "feel for" someone, particularly if they've experienced a loss of some kind. However, "empathy" means something quite different. Another way to say it is empathy means to "feel with" or "feel into" as in "feel into the other person", which has a powerful impact both for the empathizer and the person being empathized with.

Empathic Awareness Skill is something we do before we even start to communicate with someone and while we communicate with them. It's our internal perspective, our frame of mind, the lens, the heart through which we see ourselves and others. It's the way we communicate, and that is the reason I consider it to be the foundational skill for all the other skills.

Empathic Awareness Skill has 4 steps:

Step 1: Recognize your own inherent value and dignity as a person. Your inner self. Your unique value and special character.

It's vital to cultivate a self-awareness of our own personal value, such that we can honestly think to ourselves (and even say aloud), "I am unique, special, and valuable." Truly, there is no one else like you or me in all the world. We are each one of a kind with our own unique talents, abilities and personality.

"Put your own mask on first"

If we don't believe in our own value, how will we believe in the value of others? When you're on an airplane, the flight attendant tells everyone that if there is a loss in cabin air pressure the oxygen mask will drop from overhead and put yours on first before you try to help someone else; otherwise, you won't be able to breathe and you won't be much help to anyone. Similarly, if we aren't able to recognize our own value first, it will be more difficult to turn and see the value of others.

In fact, the most common teaching in the world's religions is a form of "love others as you love yourself" and even self-help professionals express forms of this teaching. However, it only works if a person loves and values him or herself. People who don't love or value themselves can actually be harmful, both to themselves and to others, because if they don't appreciate themselves then they very likely will not appreciate others.

Ways to enhance Empathic Awareness of our personal value and potential:

- **Meditation, Self-Reflection, Prayer:**

These are time-honored practices to help calm the mind and body, eliminate distractions, clear the mental and spiritual air, and connect with the deeper, positive mind within oneself— our internal essence. If you're a religious or spiritual person, this is pausing to connect to a higher power, your life source.

- **Inspirational and Motivational Books**

These words have the power to instruct, uplift and energize your thinking and bolster your sense of self and self-value. These words are food for the mind and soul. Inspirational and motivational books can help you recognize your value as well as identify and nurture your unique talents and potential.

- **Speeches, Seminars, Webinars, Workshops, Sermons:**

The more exposure we have to uplifting, thought-provoking information and testimonies from others that give us greater understanding and awareness of our own value, talents, and capacities the more we should take them and invest in them—we'll be the better for it.

- **Positive Self-Talk:**

We are what we think. Fill your mind with positive self-talk (I can do it, I'm a person of great value, and I have talents that can help others). Think positive thoughts and expectations about yourself and others, your goals, relationships, and life in general and those things are more likely to come to fruition. Norman Vincent Peale, author of the classic The Power of Positive Thinking, may have said it best: "Change your thoughts and you change your world."

On the contrary, if you fill your mind with negative self-talk (I can't, I'm no good, there's no way) then those things will likely come true. In a very real sense, we reap what we sow in our minds—positive thoughts produce positive words, actions and results; negative thoughts produce negative words, actions and results. How we direct our thinking, self-talk, and attitude determines which way we go.

Step 2: Recognize the inherent value and dignity of the other person that they are likewise worthy of respect.

As mentioned above, every human being is special, regardless of their level of income, social status or other characteristics. We are fellow travelers on this planet, in this time and space. Of all the people who are alive now, and who have ever lived or will live, the people we encounter each day are in our very presence, our sphere of awareness. We can even think there is some purpose for their being in our world—something we can learn from them, and something they can learn from us.

Each person has their strong points and weak points, faults and quirks, but also, like us, they are unique, special, and valuable—we need to see them that way, treat them that way. I suggest that this is a prerequisite to being able to have good communication, in that we are grateful for these people in our lives and can acknowledge that every single person may have something to teach us and help us grow. In fact, you might notice something special in them they don't even see in themselves.

Pause -> Reflect -> Adjust -> Act

91

I've found this to be a very helpful mantra: Pause. Reflect. Adjust. Act. It's like an inner compass helping to steer myself in the right direction. Often, in the course of the day, while I'm communicating with someone and my mind starts to drift or my sense of being empathic starts to fade, I'll catch myself and think Pause, Reflect, Adjust, and Act.

The Pause helps me stop my wayward thinking on the spot—like a stoplight. Then I Reflect on the importance of the person and what they're talking about or the situation, I Adjust my focus and intentionality to value and zero in on them and what they're saying and feeling, and finally I Act by being more empathically present.

This mantra and state of mind act as a realignment tool. Like driving a car or flying a plane, we are constantly making adjustments to stay on the path toward our destination. In this case, that destination is being empathically aware of ourselves and the other person in the moment.

"But what about a person I don't like?"

Let's face it, there are many people we may not like for one reason or another—their attitude, personality, behavior, the way they talk or dress, their breath!—but even regarding them, you can look at the bright side and think, This difficult person may be in my life so that I can: 1) grow my heart to unconditionally value him/her

Think of the people in your life that you don't particularly like—that nosy acquaintance, the relative who talks too much, your untidy neighbor, an arrogant co-worker. As much as you dislike some of their behaviors and attitudes, try looking beyond those characteristics and think, they may be a test for me to grow my heart of empathy and compassion for who they are as unique human beings.

You can also think, perhaps they agitate something in me that I need to confront and deal with—my own arrogant and judgmental attitudes, my hair-trigger anger, my prejudice, etc. Indeed, these people who are challenging for you to deal with may be an opportunity to stretch your heart and grow your character. Who knows, you may be challenging to them!

Act Loving in order to Feel Loving

Dr. Jerome Bruner, Harvard psychologist, writes, "You are more likely to act yourself into feeling than feel yourself into action." The lesson here is to act loving in order to feel loving rather than simply wait for loving feelings to emerge before you act. If we act loving and caring even to someone we don't like, the feelings of love and caring will sooner or later emerge within us. Thus, we acted ourselves into the feelings we wanted to have.

Ways we can enhance our Empathic Awareness of others:

- Think of this day as an experiment in which you see the people you come in contact with as opportunities for you to grow in love and compassion by practicing caring, understanding, patience, forgiveness and gratitude. Test the hypothesis that Empathic Awareness will work in your life today.

- Take the 1-Day Empathy Challenge! Practice seeing the people you meet today as a gift—a unique opportunity to grow your heart and empathy.

Step 3: Create the desire in your mind to want to listen and relate to them—to feel and understand them as they are.

Intentions precede actions. As we create the desire—the intention—to relate well with others because we recognize their value as unique and special human beings, that desire will fuel and mobilize our want to listen and relate to them and move us closer to doing so. We're moving from the internal realization of its importance to the external action of doing it. Cultivating such intentionality within our heart and mind is a deliberate act on our part, an act of focus and sincerity, and a vital element of the Empathic Awareness Skill.

Author Josephine Billings similarly said, "To the world you may be one person, but to one person you may be the world." The love we give another person may be the very thing that gives them hope—helps them feel their value.

We need to reach out with our eyes, ears, words, and attitude to make a connection of heart with that person. An unexpected benefit of Empathic Awareness is that in reaching to understand and relate to the deeper heart and feelings of another person this will take us deeper into our own heart, similar to getting to the same water level. Simply put, we can't get to a deeper place in someone else from a shallow place in ourselves.

Step 4: Think of the positives in your relationship with the other person—**your spouse, child, parent, friend, co-worker, etc. Even a stranger—they're in your world too!**

Thinking of the positives about other people and our relationship to them creates an attraction, a magnetic effect drawing us toward them. We're focusing on the positives, what's bright about them, rather than focusing on repelling any negatives. Our positive perspective is the key and a powerful aspect of Empathic Awareness Skill.

Ways to develop our positive perspective of others:

Focus on the good. Think of the qualities and characteristics we appreciate about them—for example, the co-worker trying their best on that particular project even though they may not always clean up after themselves in the lunchroom; our spouse or partner constantly giving us encouraging words even though they are sometimes late for appointments; the neighbor working two jobs to support his family even though their front yard looks kind of shabby. When we focus on the positives of who they are and what they do, it will help us put any negatives into better perspective, even if we need to discuss and problem-solve some of those negatives with them. Our positive attitude opens up our heart to the possibilities of what can go right instead of what can go wrong.

Chapter 9. Assertive Communication Techniques

We've covered various aspects of assertive communication, now we'll be looking at some very specific assertiveness techniques that you can implement. These are all specific examples of behaviors that assertive people demonstrate, and that can be easily applied to common situations.

Saying No

A key part of being assertive is making sure your own needs are met and your opinions are heard, without resorting to aggression. A common one that a lot of people struggle with is just saying no.

Assertive people are comfortable saying 'no.' they understand that they don't have to provide a reason, but will often provide a sound and logical reason if they do have one. The next time somebody asks you to do something that you don't want to do, try responding politely with a 'no.'

For example, if you're asked to take on extra work, but you're already swamped, you can simply say *'I'd love to be able to help, but I've got more than enough work already.'*

Ask For More Time

It's impossible to always have the information and answers you might need to hand. An assertive communicator recognizes that this is normal and simply asks for any additional time they might need.

This can be applied whether you need time to consider your feelings about a situation, or you need to research tangible facts before answering a question.

For this technique to be effective, you need to deliver your request for more time confidently and calmly. Simply state what you need the time for, and how long it will take. For example, 'I'll need to check on the facts for you, how about we reconvene tomorrow?' Or, 'I'm not sure how I feel about that. I'd like to take some time to consider it, let's discuss it again next week.'

Using 'I' Statements

This technique is best used when you want to address somebody else's behavior. Criticizing others can cause emotions to flare and can make people become defensive and unwilling to listen. One reason for this is that we tend to use blaming language when addressing other people's actions.

Using 'I' statements forces you to take responsibility for your own feelings and avoids placing blame on the other person. By using 'I' statements, you can address emotive issues without immediately putting the other person into defensive mode.

For example, instead of saying 'you're late,' you can say 'I was expecting you at two o'clock.' Instead of saying 'you always forget to lock the door,' you can say 'I get frustrated when you forget to lock the door.'

Rehearse Situations or Have a 'Script'

If a scenario makes you feel anxious, rehearsing how you might behave and respond in that situation can help. For example, if you're due to have a performance review with your manager, try playing out in your mind. Consider all the different ways it could play out, and what your manager might say along with your possible responses.

For each potential question you might be asked or challenge you think your manager might give, consider how you want to respond. Develop a loose script that you can use to answer key points. The script is simply to help you organize your thoughts, you wouldn't take an actual script into the meeting. However, by considering and rehearsing some potential responses you will reduce the anxiety you might feel. It can also prevent any potentially awkward moments where you struggle to find an appropriate response.

Be a Broken Record

This technique can be used when somebody isn't taking 'no' for an answer or is refusing to accept what you are saying to them. It's a very simple concept, where you simply repeat your initial response until the other person finally accepts it.

You can reword your response slightly each time, but you need to keep the message the same. For example, if somebody asks you to attend a party that you don't want to attend, you might respond with 'I can't make it on that day.'

If the other person doesn't accept that, challenging why you can't make it, you might simply say 'I can't make it on that day, I have a prior appointment.' If they continue to challenge, you would just repeat that you cannot make it on that day.

The key to making this work properly is to repeat yourself without displaying any anger, irritation, frustration or anxiety.

Your body language and tone should be as calm and neutral as possible. Once the other person sees that you won't change your stance, they will usually back off.

Fogging

Fogging is a technique where you accept unwarranted or malicious criticism by calmly acknowledging that there may be an element of truth to the remark, without accepting that their comment has any real merit.

It's a way to defuse a situation where someone with an aggressive style is trying to get a reaction from you. Instead of the expected reaction of refuting the criticism or becoming upset, you simply calmly respond with a mild acknowledgment that sidesteps their aggressive intent.

For example, if someone says 'Why did you take that route? That was a stupid thing to do!' You might respond with 'Yes, I could have taken a different route and arrived quicker.'

Negative Inquiry

Negative inquiry is another way of deflecting criticism by asking questions instead of arguing or becoming defensive.

Again, the key is to do this is a very calm and non-confrontational manner, without sarcastic tone, so that your attempt at assertive negative inquiry isn't mistaken for passive-aggression.

Active Voice

Assertive people use the active voice more frequently than the passive voice. Active voice is when it is very clear exactly who is performing an action.

For example, 'The report must be delivered today' is an example of passive voice, because it isn't clear who is completing the action of delivering the report. 'James must deliver the report today,' is the active voice, because it is very clear who is expected to deliver the report. A simple test of whether something is active or passive is to add 'by zombies' to the end of the sentence. If it still makes sense, the sentence is passive.

Consider the following sentences:

I was taught to stand correctly (by zombies)

I learned to drive (by zombies)

The report has been written already (by zombies)

Jane already wrote the report (by zombies)

A and C are passive voice, because the addition of 'by zombies' doesn't make the sentence incorrect, whereas B and D are active voice. By choosing to use the active voice, assertive people avoid ambiguity and misunderstandings.

Set Clear Boundaries

If you struggle to set boundaries, then other people will find it easy to walk all over you. Assertive people are clear about their boundaries and they set them clearly, If their boundaries are overstepped, they reassert them quickly.

By not being afraid to stand up for themselves and challenge people who try to push their boundaries, assertive people protect their self-esteem and earn respect from others.

Address Specific Behaviors

Assertive people don't shy away from addressing issues, but when they do they focus on criticizing the behavior and not the person. By focusing on the specific behavior, they allow the other person to understand exactly what needs to change, and allow them to take on board the feedback without feeling personally attacked.

This works best when combined with 'I' statements and delivered in a calm and non-confrontational manner.

By implementing these techniques and the other information within this, you will begin to become a more assertive communicator. So far, we've focused specifically on verbal communication, although some of these techniques can be applied to written communication as well.

However, in our modern world we frequently communicate in writing. Emails, texts, messenger apps, social media are often daily occurrences, and they can have very different rules and etiquette than the more formal medium of letters.

We'll take a look at how the different methods of written communication vary from verbal communication, and how to apply assertive communication techniques to those methods.

Chapter 10. Tips for Communicating Effectively In Every Aspect of Your Life

In order to develop healthy communication skills, it is crucial that you become ready to completely shed your old skin and turn into a new person altogether. Sticking to your old self won't help since communication requires you to open up and spread out as much as possible. After you promise yourself this change, follow the following tips to develop your own set of excellent communication skills:

Listen

It may sound absurd, but it's a proven fact that in order to speak well, the first thing you need to master is the art of listening. Listening, and not hearing. However, not everyone is good at listening. We end up missing out on a lot of information due to our absent-mindedness and ignorance. If only we dedicated even fifty percent of our attention to listening to what others had to say, then we'd be owners of more and better knowledge than what we do today.

Everyone hears, very few listen. The first step to good communication is listening. It's only when you hear the other party that you grasp how to respond. Blabber on your own track and you fail to be a communicator from the very start.

Speak

Ever since man's stopped using sign language to communicate, speaking has dominated his usage of tongue to convey information. What would you call speaking? Using words to send relevant data? Speaking has evolved into more than the mere sending of words.

Speaking is the use of the tongue to convey emotions, intentions and information to other people. It helps you make others understand what you want, know or feel. If it were not for speaking, humans would have still used hand gestures to show they are hungry, sleepy or sexually aroused. Just imagine such a scenario.

Speaking opens not only your mouth but also your mind. The action of speaking requires and pushes you to think. Thinking is an activity that keeps you engaged mentally. When you think, you naturally develop and sharpen your mind. Your mind opens shut doors to let you think and speak. You then start accepting new ways to form opinions and to put them out for others to see.

There is no limit to your wings of imagination. You start exploring new dimensions and seeing better ways to perceive people. Basically, you change your personality in such a manner that others notice changes in you. Speaking therefore, opens you up. It removes fetters from your development and lets you witness the best you can achieve. Speaking is an art, which when mastered, covers almost more than half of your communication skills.

Mind your Body Language

Your body language speaks more about you than you do with your tongue. The way you come across as a person is as much determined by your body language as by your words and looks.

Body language could be defined as a combination of all those physical activities that you unintentionally perform that depicts your intentions and emotions. The amount of communication you perform by your body language is almost equivalent to the amount you perform by what you say.

The following is an example of how body language is as good a communication medium as any other:

Susie is an average office worker in a reputed company. Her boss relies upon her skills and gives her regular tasks to perform. Despite the corporate skills she possesses, she is a poor communicator. When she is assigned a task in person from her boss, she smiles and shows acceptance while being fully aware that the assigned work is beyond her capacity. Having accepted the task, she moves on to complete it in the given time frame and completes it very poorly. Though her work is not done well, the devotion that would have made it satisfactory was noticed as missing.

The language of her body conveyed competence while the real picture was something completely different. What she showed from her physical actions didn't match the frequency of what she was capable of. Such a difference in body language and the real picture creates issues.

Communication is an untapped art that when mastered would reap you unimaginable benefits. You won't end up making false promises. You avoid unnecessary friction in life by clearly stating things. There comes clarity in what you intend to do and what you are capable of doing. Your intentions are unequivocally expressed, and your motives truly revealed. Body language is merely a tool to properly convey your message without resorting to words.

Communication isn't always vocal. It assumes different forms like eye movements, talking style, hand gestures and general hand movements. Body language is a good way to avoid using words and ensuring the quick sending of messages. It's easy and smart to communicate without putting any special effort into it. Talking is good, sure, but what if you had better options to convey information? Body language is the answer.

Spice up

Everyone speaks. But those who leave an impression behind in their listeners' minds are the ones remembered. Simply constructed sentences and casually picked up words hardly do justice to a speaker's image. When you do not infuse life into your words, you fail to impress those listening. By life, I mean excitement, appeal and class. When you make your conversations funny, witty and sarcastic, you open new doors of possibilities.

So how do you go about spicing up your conversations? If there's a possibility for a fun angle being added to your sentences, go for it. Do not hesitate to imagine well and imbibe the said imagination into your words. Cleverly selected words have more magic than casually said ones.

Briefness is another character that elevates your conversation's worth. The briefer your sentences, the greater the impact you leave behind. A study found that shorter sentences have more conviction powers than longer ones. When you wrap up your conversations with short sentences, you allow the other party to think back-something that is not possible with long sentences. When you allow the listeners to think upon what you have just said, they realize it makes sense.

On the contrary, when you do not allow such time, they assume you are either bluffing or trying to dominate the proceedings. Shorter sentences, therefore, enhance your impact as a communicator.

Sarcasm is a trait not everyone possesses. It is the rare quality to whiplash someone without them knowing that you have just owned them. The quality of sarcasm is a funny way to get back at those opposite you. If you master the quality well, you could enter into any argument blind folded. Though seen as a last resort in a debate, it serves its purpose when you want to make the opposite party regret locking horns with you. Being a good communicator requires the inculcation of the characteristic of sarcasm in your skills set.

Another quality that needs to be possessed by you in order for you to turn into a good communicator is humor. Humor never fails to entertain listeners. If you have this trait on your side, you will not only end up making your point but also make the audience laugh. However, when you communicate, you should guard against excessive or negative humor. Humor in excess dilutes the conversation and shifts the direction from your conversation to fun. The very purpose of having a conversation is defeated. Negative humor is that which offends race, gender, and similar sensitive issues. Refrain from using negative humor in your communication as it will show you in a bad light. The point you are trying to make not only fades away but is also misunderstood.

A good conversation involves both the parties-the speaker and the listener. Both the parties are accorded equal importance and neither predominates over the other. If this balance is disturbed, a conversation steers away from its purpose. Such a balance is mandatory for any conversation to achieve an ideal stage from whence it receives not only acknowledgement but also applause from the audience.

When an already perfect conversation is infused with things like fun, sarcasm, witticism and intellect, the impact such a conversation has on its listeners is huge. A bland and dry conversation is only informative. But a conversation that is infused with the traits does more than inform. It keeps the parties excited and informed. It makes them crave for more and never bores them throughout the conversation. The communication you perform this way is an ideal one.

Read

Reading is a habit that when inculcated in a human reaps him/her numerous benefits. When you read, you explore the world. New doors of shining experiences are opened, and you start seeing things through other people's perspectives. You are not limited anymore when it comes to mental faculties. You become more familiar with people, their views and their way of thinking. Reading familiarizes you with images that you never thought would be possible.

It is vital to encourage the habit of reading at a young age. When children are taught to not just learn reading but also keep continuing it, they have a particular thing to return to. With age, this habit turns into a hobby and children then start exploring various genres. Be it fiction or autobiographies, they cannot keep their hands off books in general. They squeal upon coming across a bookshop and spend all their pocket money on buying books. The art of buying second-hand is more pronounced in your children than it may be in you. Tender minds are like clean slates. Whatever you write on them will stay for a long time in their lives. When you introduce children to such a healthy habit, you essentially push them towards being a good communicator.

How does reading help one become a good communicator?

Communication doesn't take place in a vacuum. It requires a sender to send across a message to the receiver. But what is the source of such information? What if such information is not in turn received, but demands creation?

A piece of communication could be regarding an idea or a piece of art. Now such an idea must have been thought of by someone. Or this piece of art must have been created by someone. Where does the experience required to create such things come from? It's from reading books and experiencing things that you receive the skills that get employed to facilitate communication.

Reading introduces you to different worlds with their own colorful dimensions. When you read, you see new possibilities and events. If it's fictional, the imagination so employed in creating it is really helpful in transferring you to a different realm. You gain not only literary experiences but also imaginative ones. You get equipped to spread your wings of imagination and dive into the vast world of communication.

The perusal of books familiarizes you with ideas and probabilities. These ideas and probabilities push you to think. When you think, you automatically get qualified to engage yourself in communication.

Socialize

When you meet new people, you pick up their stories and experiences. Everyone has learnt a lot of lessons from their lives. When they share it with others, they allow them to become a part of their stories. By becoming a part of their stories, you learn the lessons they learnt. The very essence of communication is that it is to be facilitated by at least one party. When you are the one doing it, you need to pick up the social courage to do it. If you shy away from social company, you are killing any chances of socializing, and hence by extension, communication.

Socialization is the art of mingling with society. It requires you to gel well with those who are not a part of your family. You may know your family members very well but that's not the case with others.

Chapter 11. Tips on How to Be Highly Effective in Communication and Public Speaking

One of the most significant indicators of a powerful communicator is someone who can engagingly put across their point when addressing an audience. Whether you are giving a presentation to a boardroom full of people or talking to a broad audience from a podium, some valuable pointers can help you communicate more effectively when it comes to driving home important points. Are you able to persuade and convince people of your idea? Are you able to express yourself compellingly on a public platform? Are you able to communicate with a group of people without any space for misunderstanding?

Here are 7 power packed tips to transform into a highly effective and articulate public speaker.

1. Grab Attention with a Powerful Beginning and End

This doesn't go on to say everything in between should be mediocre. It just means your beginning should be powerful enough to get your audience hooked and listening intently to the rest of the speech. Don't begin with some nondescript and uninspiring like "Today I am going to talk about so and so." It is plain, insipid and boring, and doesn't encourage your audience to listen any further.

Instead, begin with a shocking or unexpected statistic, an incredible statement, an interesting anecdote or a powerful quotation. The idea is to induce shock and interest to grab your audience's attention. Don't make it unnecessarily scandalous though, just include an element of surprise.

Similarly, while concluding the speech, offer a summary of all the important points made during the speech to reinforce what you've said, eliminating any misunderstandings. Also, close with a powerful statement or quotation that your audience is likely to remember for long. Make it unique and memorable!

2. Work with a Script but Don't Read Looking at It

I always recommend creating a rough skeleton of what you plan to say in the speech. It can include important points you wish to address or quotations/anecdotes you want to use during the speech. We are human, and there is a tendency to forget things. Work with a rough script or draft and keep building upon it as you speak. This will invariably come when you go with the flow of the speech and gauge audience reaction.

However, don't ever read from a script. Use it only as a prompt. One of the most powerful ways of connecting with your audience involves looking them in the eye and speaking. You will come across as more credible and drive home the point more effectively. If you need to look into the paper for clues, simply glance at it and then convey it to your audience by looking them in the eye. Never ever read verbatim from your notes. It makes you come across as a highly ineffective communicator.

By maintaining eye contact with your audience, you focus on the message. Create a brief and rough outline to keep on track with the speech but always communicate by maintaining eye contact with your audience. The speakers who read directly from a script make themselves appear highly ineffectual. There is no eye contact, and as a speaker, you don't come across as passionate in the points you are making. You won't light up your audience or lead them to action. It goes without saying that you need a powerful opening and closing and should have these points prepared. However, you also need to speak from your heart.

Instead of utilizing a verbatim script, use index cards for preparing your speech. Write a few words or a brief phrase on the cards to offer clues about the main idea, concept or story that you can speak about confidently.

3. Personalize and Humanize the Message

I am not lying here. I literally sleep through speeches that are clinical, staccato-like and boring. Unless your audience is a bunch of machines, avoid making your speech mechanical. As a presenter, you'll get plenty of brownie points for personalizing the message. Irrespective of the topic, there's always a way to personalize and humanize a message. It's a wonderful way to get intimate and build a connection with your audience. People relate better to stories or anecdotes, experiences of other people, stories of hope and triumphs, tragedies and challenges and more.

Add a dash of humor, however serious the topic, to make it more appealing for your audience. Stories and real-life incidents will add an element of credibility to keep your listeners hooked. Share personal views and opinions to make it more human, while avoiding controversial statements all the same. When you state your preferences or state your opinion, you come across as more human, which allows your audience to connect with you on a deeper level. Use personal interest stories and elements throughout the speech. This technique makes it easy for the audience to warm up to the speaker.

All the same, you will conquer any feelings of nervousness and anxiety, while experiencing greater ease by connecting with your audience on a deeper level. Just like your audience warms up to you, you will warm up to them. Any lingering nervousness will be overcome when you make the speech more personal. Focus on building a relationship with your audience.

4. Strengthen Your Vocal Delivery

Your voice is your power. Use it to your advantage by throwing it in the most effective manner. Your voice is one of the most flexible tools when it comes to communicating with your audience in a compelling and effective way. You can add plenty of effects, coloration, and emotions to the voice by modulating it to express the right emotions and feelings. Don't speak in a monotone or single flat tone. Use plenty of variation to make your speech more varied. It adds more punch to the speech.

For example, when you want to make a powerful statement, start on a flat note. Later, raise your pitch, and end on a flat note all over again. Don't stop on a high pitch since that makes your statement appears more like a question. End on a flat note, so it seems like you are making a powerful statement rather than a question. You can work with a speech coach if you want to make your presentation skills even more power-packed.

5. Body Language

Your body is a potent communication tool that helps convey what you are trying to say by adding more depth to your message. Through your physical expression, you will put across your point even more convincingly to the audience. What do you think are an actor's secrets of commanding the stage or leading the audience to believe something that they want them to feel? The power of body language!

Use your body language to your advantage by maintaining the right power positions throughout the speech. Understand the fact that, other than what you are verbally speaking, you are also communicating with your audience on a subconscious level through non-verbal clues. There are subtle signals being sent to them through your body language, tone, voice and more. Body language is essential because it helps complement your verbal message to ensure there is no misunderstanding or that the message is conveyed more compellingly.

Always stand while delivering a speech. Your full body form should be visible to the audience if you want them to take you seriously and come across as authoritative. Your position on the podium or room, your body movements, your hand gestures— everything adds to the speech power.

Ground yourself firmly on the podium by assuming a dominant stance. Your feet should be spread at the armpit width, while the body weight should be evenly spread. Assuming this posture offers you the feeling of stability. You will appear more balanced, credible and trustworthy. Your audience will be more likely to accept your ideas when they subconsciously perceive you to be more grounded.

Your arms should be in a neutral position. When you are self-conscious while speaking, you'll do a lot of things with the arms except leaving them unnoticed at your sides. Begin with a neutral position by keeping your arms at your sides. Next, use your hands to gesticulate while speaking. It will add more punch to the message. Don't cross or lock your arms, it is a sign of physically blocking yourself from the audience or creating a barrier.

Use more open body postures, which will make you come across as a transparent, open, credible and trustworthy person. Don't keep your hand anywhere near the upper body. That part of your body should be open so that there is no barrier between you and the audience.

If you are sitting and delivering a speech, sit straight and bend slightly forward. Bring your back about one third ahead on the seat, and then lean forward slightly with the upper body! You'll appear more authoritative, professional, engaging and credible when you lean ahead. Leaning back or slouching makes you uncomfortable and isn't useful when it comes to delivering the message in a convincing manner.

Your gestures should be animated and should complement the point you're trying to make. Don't use your hands excessively; use them effectively. Gestures are meant to emphasize the point you are trying to drive home more powerfully. It can be used for amplifying your message and lending it more purpose. For example, saying "you" is not enough but saying "you" and pointing to the audience makes all the difference in emphasizing or amplifying the "you."

While some speakers have the habit of randomly wandering about the podium or stage, others stride in a more purposeful manner. Move with a greater sense of purpose and mindfulness. Know that every step you take adds to your message. Before you begin speaking about a new point, take a few steps. The movement will make the audience sit up and take notice.

6. Don't Overlook Q & A

Q & A is your best opportunity to persuade your audience when putting across your point in a compelling and persuasive manner even after the presentation is done. However, there can be plenty of questions and challenges. Speakers have an opportunity during Q & A to indulge in self-depreciating humor, rephrase the presentation, and summarize the speech to ensure there is no further misunderstanding.

Allow your audience to throw questions for greater clarity. Ask questions to check your audience's level of understanding. Avoid pointing a finger in the direction of the person who has asked the question. Instead, keep your palms open or maintain an open stance to communicate your point of view to the audience effectively and compellingly. Use Q & A to keep the audience hooked to your side.

7. Avoid Confusing Topic with Purpose

To begin with, even the best speakers confuse topic and objective/purpose. If you ask them the objective of their talk, they'll say they are going to talk about so and so topic. However, that is merely their topic, not the purpose of their speech. The purpose of their presentation is what they are trying to achieve through it. Do you want to persuade the audience into thinking like you? Do you want to sell something to them? Are you trying to gauge audience preferences or interests?

Information or topic is what you are going to share, but your objective will establish a structure for sharing that information. Gaining more clarity of purpose will help you create your presentation more effectively. Each time you start preparing a rough draft for your presentation, begin with a clear objective in mind. Once your purpose or intention is established, it is easy to work around how you are going to achieve it. I always say this—if your "why" is clear, your "how" will find a way.

Chapter 12. How to Use the FORD Method to Keep Any Conversation Alive

We've all been there. You're talking to someone, everything seems to be going well…and then the conversation shows signs of slowing down, or even stopping altogether. Luckily, there's one little acronym that will save you every time.

Remember – FORD

What do people enjoy talking about the most? Themselves, of course! Even the most considerate among us appreciate the chance to air our opinions and share our life experiences. When you run out of things to say, just think FORD.

F - Family

This is a universally relevant topic of conversation. After all, everyone has a family. Even if they are estranged from their relatives or have a poor relationship with them, it all counts! However, take it slow. Jumping in with a question like, "So, do you get on well with your family?" will make you seem a bit too intense. Instead, direct the conversation to the topic in such a manner that it doesn't seem forced.

You can do this by mentioning your own family. For instance, suppose you were taking a class taught by a professor who reminded you of your eccentric Uncle Andrew. You could mention this fact casually if you wanted to provide a natural bridge into a conversation about relatives.

You could say, "You know, our professor really reminds me of my Uncle Andrew – they're both really fond of speaking ridiculously loudly!" This provides a natural opener for a discussion about families in general, quirky relatives, and so on.

Another way you can direct the topic to family is by mentioning a relevant news story. For example, you could say something like, "You know, there's this new study out that says elder siblings are smarter than their younger brothers and sisters." Most people would take the opportunity to respond in the context of their own experiences.

For instance, your conversation partner might say, "Well, I don't believe that! I have an older sister, but she's as dumb as a rock!" This would provide you with an opportunity to ask further questions about the number of siblings they have, why they think their sister is dumb, and so on.

Of course, you need to remember that some people have a history of family trauma and may not want to talk about the subject at all. If you get the impression they are at all uncomfortable, back off and transition to another topic.

Should the two of you become friends, the subject will probably come up at a later date, and they may feel happier sharing more of their background once they feel safe around you.

O - Occupation

Almost everyone has an occupation. Asking what someone does for a living is fairly safe, because most of us have been raised to think that it is a socially appropriate question. However, don't make the mistake of asking a series of obvious questions that put someone on the spot. Whilst asking questions is a sign of interest, and is generally a good strategy, you risk entering into interrogation mode or "interview mode" if you aren't careful.

For example, let's say that you have been introduced to a woman and ask her what she does for a living. She tells you that she is a nurse. In this situation, most people would then throw a volley of questions, such as:

"Do you work with adults or children?"

"How long have you been working as a nurse?"

"Where did you go to school?"

"Do you work night shifts, day shifts, or a mixture of both?"

The trouble with this approach is that it comes across as quite intense. It's better to ask the other person what they do for a living, give a thoughtful response to their reply, and then let the conversation develop naturally.

To continue with the nurse example, a comment such as, "Oh wow, I've always admired nurses. It looks like a really pressured job, and I guess you need to make important decisions every day," would be a good response.

Quite often, you won't have to launch into interview mode if you give this kind of reply, because the other person will feel compelled to either build on what you have said, or correct you. This results in a natural conversation and better rapport.

If your conversation partner is not in work, you can take the same approach when asking about their college classes or what they like to do in their spare time. *Under no circumstances should you make clichéd jokes or remarks about someone else's occupation.*

They've heard them all before, and you will only make yourself look foolish. For example, no lawyer wants to hear yet another reference to ambulance chasing, and no vet wants to hear another "joke" about killing people's pets.

R - Recreation

Aside from work or study, what does everyone do? Engage in hobbies or pursue their interests, of course! Recreation can be a conversational goldmine if you seize the opportunity. Much like jobs and college courses, recreation is an area that people expect to crop up in conversation. It's therefore acceptable to simply ask, "What do you like to do in your free time?"

Don't panic if someone mentions an obscure hobby, or an interest that doesn't appeal to you in the slightest. Admit that you know nothing about their hobby but make it clear that you want to know more about their lives and experiences. Say something like, "Oh, I don't know much about that, but I know that people who do it tend to love it! What do you most like about it?" Even if you aren't in a position to understand what they are actually talking about, you can still build rapport by asking about their feelings.

Occasionally, you might meet someone who is too busy working to enjoy any hobbies. These people value their work above everything else – even if they don't actually like doing it – and have few other interests in life. (Resist any urge you might have to tell them that their work-life balance needs some adjustment, because they won't listen.)

There are two approaches you can take when talking to a workaholic about their hobbies and interests. If they seem to enjoy their job, make that the focus of conversation instead. If not, ask them what they would like to do if they had any free time.

D - Dreams

This is probably the most personal of the four topics, but if you can hold a meaningful conversation about someone's dreams, they will feel kindly towards you. Why? Because most people harbor some kind of ambition or secret longing, but rarely get the chance to share them with someone else.

Human beings want to be understood and validated. Therefore, if you can listen to someone's dreams in a nonjudgmental manner, and even encourage them to pursue them, they will think you a first-rate conversationalist!

Don't dive straight in by asking someone, "So, do you have any secret dreams or unfulfilled ambitions?" You need to take a subtler route. For example, you could use one of their hobbies or interests as a springboard, and make an educated guess as to what their dream might be.

If someone mentions that they love to read contemporary fiction and write short stories, ask them whether they have ever thought of becoming a professional author. It doesn't matter whether your guess is correct, because it will move the conversation along regardless.

Another option is to move the conversation in a more existential direction. Ask them a question that prompts them to think, "What's it all about?" Mention an event that made an impact on you, and tell them that sometimes you start to wonder whether you should be taking your own dreams more seriously.

This usually sets up a conversation about unfulfilled ambitions. You could take a more direct approach and tell them about something on your bucket list that you plan to do later in the year. This allows you to ask a question like, "Do you have a bucket list?" If they do, ask them what's on it. If they don't, ask them what they'd most like to achieve before their time on earth is up.

Getting the Most from the FORD Strategy

The four FORD topics are universal. They allow you to have a conversation with anyone from young children to the elderly, and everyone in between. However, they are most powerful when you use them to probe beyond the surface, and discover what really makes someone who they are.

The more you focus on feelings and meaning rather than facts, the greater the rapport, and the more meaningful the conversation. Don't worry if the conversation takes an unexpected turn of events – these topics are intended as starting points that work well as points of discussion in their own right, but can easily develop into a fascinating exchange of experiences and views. The key is to avoid bombarding someone with questions, and to maintain a fair balance by offering a similar amount of information about yourself.

Bonus Topics for Conversation

The FORD strategy gives you four broad areas you can mine for conversation, but there are a few more topics that can work to keep a dialogue going.

Current affairs: Once upon a time, people could make a choice to completely avoid the news. All they had to do was avoid newspapers and news programs. We don't really have that choice any more – major issues of the day pop up as trends on social media, and almost every lifestyle site at least touches on current affairs.

This is great news for you, because it means that almost everyone you talk to will have at least a vague idea of what is happening in the world. It isn't a good idea to watch the regular news too often – there's far too much negativity in most mainstream media – but keeping up to date with the headlines will help you find common ground in conversation. Try these phrases:

"Hey, did you happen to read about….?" "So I was reading about [insert interesting event here – preferably something positive]. What do you think about that?"

"[Interesting topic] is trending on Twitter/Instagram/other social media platform today, did you happen to see it?"

One word of warning – if you are going to talk about anything remotely related to politics or religion, consider your audience.

Be prepared to divert the topic if it turns out that you hit upon one of their red-button issues.

If you have the suspicion that whoever you are talking to holds views that are rather different from your own, it's best to stick to lighter subjects. If in doubt, talk about the weather, celebrities, movies, sporting events, or any other issue that won't generate too much controversy. Don't let the conversation degenerate into a fight.

Pets: Lots of people own pets, and those who don't often wish they did. Pet owners form strong bonds with their animals. If you've ever heard a dog owner talk for half an hour about the way Fluffy likes to sit on the couch and bark along with the radio (yes, I have had this experience), you'll know that pets can be a gateway to a lengthy conversation. You can ask someone whether they have any pets, and if so, what they are like. Other avenues to explore include pets your family owned when you were growing up, and what pets you would like to own.

Your surroundings: This works in almost any situation. Quite simply, you find something notable about the location in which you are interacting with the other person, and comment on it.

Chapter 13. Communication Levels

Communicating with others happen on several different levels; each one has its own complexities and nuances. The levels that communication happens on are verbal, physical, emotional, auditory, and energetic.

These five levels of communication have been known for a while, but most people aren't even aware of them. Understanding them is can be very helpful when a person is trying to improve their communication skills.

Level One: Verbal Communication

While this may be the most obvious level of human communication, people will likely spend their entire life trying to master it. This is the level where are words are kept and are based upon the understanding of meaning between the listener and speaker. There are several different definitions for the majority of words, and very few people have the same meanings for every word.

There are different words that create different memories, meanings, and images for different people. The reasoning and logic behind a statement or argument can influence how effectively the message is received.

There are several different types of communication skills. This can be obvious things like listening and speaking clearly, to subtle things like clarifying and reflecting.

Listening and effective speaking are the basic forms of verbal communication. Effective speaking requires three things: the words, how they are said, and how they are reinforced. All of these put together affect how the message is shared and how the listeners receive and understand the message.

It is definitely worth your time to make sure that you choose your words carefully. Given the situation, you may have to choose certain words. For example, the things that you say to your coworker are going to be different than how you present an idea to executives.

Through your verbal communication, you can also add reinforcement. Reinforcement means that you use encouraging words as well as other nonverbal gestures like head nods, a smile, or eye contact. This helps to create rapport and lets the other person know that you want them to continue talking.

In order to communicate effectively on this level, you have to make sure that you use the correct words for the conversation and context, which also includes religious, ethnic, and moral differences. You must make sure you are concise and clear. Whenever you find it possible, create your thoughts before speaking so that you don't ramble. This can be an art in itself.

Level Two: Physical Communication

With the inception of NLP, neuro-linguistic programming added more importance on the visual cues of our communication. Visual cues, such as expressions, posture, breathing, stance, movement, gestures, and eye contact, play a big part in how we communicate and feel.

When a person uses techniques like mirroring and matching others gestures and posture, with integrity, it can increase the person's receptivity of the message. Physical communication works by complimenting verbal communication and can provide you with amazing results when you combine the two effectively. There are certain jobs and professions where your physical communication ability is important.

For example, in most sporting events, being able to understand and use gestures and signs is necessary. Within security agencies, it is an important skill to understand considering the nature of the job. The military and police use these skills in order to keep from being detected by enemies. Investigators and detectives will use these skills in order to figure out if somebody is lying.

In order to be a good communication on a physical level, it helps to physically match yourself up with others. You need to connect them in movement and form. It can also help you watch your hand movements, expressions, and posture.

Level Three: Auditory Communication

The sound of the voice, as well as the speed, volume, range, and tone, plays a part in how the message is received and interpreted by the listener. For example, if you are a fast talker, you may find that helpful to slow down your speech when speaking to somebody who is introverted and thoughtful; otherwise, you run the risk of not being understood.

The way that you inflect, place emphasis, and enunciate certain words will affect the way in which a person interprets what you are saying. Auditory communication is very common in other animals, such as the rattlesnake. When you hear the rattle of their tail, you know that you should probably move away. Birds are another species that puts a lot of importance on auditory communication.

In order to communicate effectively on this level, make sure that you are aware of the different auditory cues. Try to talk to others in a way that is similar to how they talk.

Level Four: Emotional Communication

There are very few people who appreciate how effective our emotional state is when we communicated and how messages are interpreted by the listener. Aristotle's pathos shows us an appeal to the audience's emotions.

Do you tend to be more receptive to a person who is life-affirming and positive or a person who is more critical? Do you like listening to boring people or enthusiastic people?

The emotions of the speaker put the listener in a certain state of mind and influences how they interpret what has been said. If you make sure that you are emotionally aware, then you will be able to communicate more efficiently because you will be able to notice the emotions of your listeners. This gives you a chance to change the conversation if need be to help make them more receptive.

In order to communicate well on this level, it is important that you become more aware of your emotional state, learn to pause, and get rid of negative emotions before you try to connect with another person. Words that are delivered with fear, pride, or anger rarely end up being received well.

Level Five: Energetic Communication

Sometimes referred to as psychic communication, this type of communication includes a large range of unseen factors, which includes consciousness, harmonics or frequency of the message, and other types of more subtle energy.

There are some people who appear to have some unique presence that can naturally provide a person with a clear message so that they understand it easily and are receptive to it.

Every living creature, on some level, is communicating through energy and vibrations, and we, for the most part, don't even notice it. Think about this: when people are placed in amongst horses, the horses will respond to a person's energy. If they feel that the person is afraid of horses, they are likely going to stay away from them.

These energies that we can read from others are influenced by emotions, much like the last level. Whether you know it or not, there have probably been things you have backed out of or declined to do something based on the "vibe" you got from somebody. That's why you want to make sure you aren't sending out "no" vibes when you want to communicate with a person.

In order to communicate well on this level, it is important that you hold high intentions for your listener's wellbeing. This is going to require a very good level of mindfulness that is typically cultivated through the practice of compassion. When you make sure that you are centered in a state of mastery, it is more likely that you will be able to access this dimension that holds a lot of insight into others, which will help you to communicate more easily.

All five levels have to be put together to be an effective communicator. The verbal level is the things we say. The physical, energetic, auditory, and emotional levels are how we convey our message.

They are all interdependent because each level affects the next. For example, how we feel emotionally is going to affect our body language and the overall field influences our emotions. Simply noticing these things can be helpful.

When we are able to spot the complexities within human communication, we can become more patient in how we talk with others and, in turn, become more compassionate towards ourselves and others.

Chapter 14. How to Use Eye Contact for Better Communication

Your eyes give your spoken messages credence. They give the message much of its meaning, and influence whether the listener believes and trusts the message.

In conversation, who gives the other person, the listener or the speaker more direct eye contact? More often than not, it's the listener (as long as that person makes an effort to listen).

What's the eye-speaker doing? The speaker often looks at the person he is talking to but quite often his eyes wander about collecting thoughts about what to say next. Others are also

- Looking skyward

- Looking at the floor

- Looking over the shoulder. Almost looking right within themselves

The assertive-speaking eye-contact technique functions differently: when delivering the message, you have a constant and genuine eye contact with the other person. Here's how you use this tool:

MAKE CONSTANT EYE CONTACT. When you talk to them, the idea is to look at the men. The secret is steady eye contact. Still, steady does not mean constant. There are anticipated and natural blinding and occasional glimpses away. Add a touch of honesty to your looks, and attract the attention of people to you and to your message. This subtle tool has a strong and positive effect.

Give it a try. Ask someone to get your letter, and twice send it to them. Make it a two to three sentence short message and start by saying, "It's something that's important to me. ."Tell your message first when you send a steady eye contact; then repeat the exact same message as you look away most of the time. Ask your test subject to let you know what message would elicit a more favorable response.

Which form responded the other person more favorably to? You can each time find steady eye contact wins. People listen less when there's little eye contact with the speaker. Their attention wanders. But the effect becomes magnetic when the constant eye contact is preserved. It draws the attention of people to you and allows them to respond to your message.

MAINTAIN EYE CONTACT. People often ask how long you can keep in touch with your eyes. Sure there is no set time for holding the eye contact and then looking away briefly. There are no rules for life and relationships. Rather, the more familiar and comfortable a relationship you have with someone, the longer the eye contact for either party can be sustained without any discomfort. Generally speaking, eye contact can vary easily from 6 to 20 seconds in one-on - one encounters, whereas in group situations, the time is less per person— three to six seconds— because you want to reach everyone within the group.

LOOK IN THE RIGHT PLACES. Look straight into the face of your audience, close to your eyes. Looking up and down the face takes less focus from the audience, and can make the listener uncomfortable.

AVOIDING EYE-CONTACT PITFALLS

When you talk to others, avoid eye-contact behaviors which make your message less than assertive, such as:

STARING AND GLARING: this form of eye contact locks in and often has a threatening feeling. These gestures are often perceived as being violent, which is far too powerful for any post. Starting and simultaneously looking below face level causes discomfort and may even offend the listener.

LOOKING AWAY AND ALL AROUND: This is the most common pitfall for speakers when it comes to eye contact. Whether they're looking for their thoughts or being deeply immersed in their messages, speakers who have little or no eye contact cause listeners to drift away.

Speakers who mostly look down when addressing someone else — especially when the message is about a sensitive issue— lower their messages ' importance. As if you can't stand firmly behind your own post, it places you on the nonassertive track.

DARTING GLANCES: unexpected glances to and from the listener. You make the receiver believe you are looking at something special or missing something else. Darting looks usually create a distraction for the listener, who then loses your message   emphasis.

BLINKING EXCESSIVELY: Blinking is a normal eye feature. However, when they do it so rapidly and often that the blinking is heard it causes a diversion for the listener. It can make your audience feel nervous about what you're supposed to say. When, in the blink of an eye, you just hint at a take that you don't have confidence in your post, the receiver does, too.

FOCUSING IN ONE PERSON, NOT EVERYONE: This behavior, like meetings, occurs in group situations. It's one thing to be talking to someone who asked you a question. But, if your eye contact remains with only one person, giving no eye contact to the rest of your audience, the other listeners feel isolated and left out, which usually creates frustration and prevents them from really listening to your message.

GLAZING OVER: This is perfect for donuts and hams but it's not good for conversation. It occurs often when you are too absorbed in your own thoughts, or when you lose your train of thought. Once it's not a big deal, but during a conversation, it has happened more than that and you seem to have tuned your own message. If you're not doing so yourself, don't expect others to turn in.

YOUR BODY IS TALKING; MAKE SURE IT'S SUPPORTING YOUR MESSAGE

Body language applies to all that you do with your body to convey your message like facial expressions, stance and movements. The concept behind assertive speech is to include these various gestures and signs in your message; that is, to come alive when you talk.

USING BODY LANGUAGE TO MAKE PASSING YOUR MESSAGE EFFECTIVE

You must decide what to do with your face and body when you speak: you can use them or hold them asleep. You can use them in assertive terms in ways that engage others positively in your message and allow you to come across as confident, animated and relaxed.

Trust means a sense of certainty in what you've got to say. Animated means that while you say it, you're alive. And comfortable means you are at ease when you speak. No one wants to listen for a long time to a person who is confused, stiff and uptight. Here's how the body-language method is used:

- **POSTURE:** Posture is how you're holding and positioning yourself. Sit down and face your receiver as an assertive way of expressing your message. Often leaning a little forward is also beneficial. Many significant communications arise while you're alone — or ought to be, if not. Sit up in your chair right now if you would like. What are you feeling? You are more attentive. Move a little forward with your post and you've got a more commanding presence to go with. Sitting up helps put your voice in a strong position too. So meeting the audience straight on encourages you to engage him or her positively.

- **FACIAL EXPRESSIONS:** Technically, when talking, you can't see your face unless you're wearing a mirror and holding it up to you. You can nevertheless feel what your face is doing. You probably know when you smile, when you have a worried look, or when you have a strong feeling about something. Your expression conveys those feelings to others. The idea of being assertive in expressing yourself is to show positive life through facial expressions. You may have heard an expression putting a smile in your face. Smiling is about making others sound more upbeat as he or she speaks.

With a smile, the muscles within your face change and help pick up your voice's inflection. That is the premise. Have the facial expressions that suit what you say in your letter. Doing so adds trust and honesty to your message— a double dose that positively inspires people to want to listen to you. Your facial expressions have a significant impact on how people interpret messages from you. Really, just check this out. Tell someone to get your message twice, and send it twice to them. Make it a two or three sentence short message and start by saying, "It's something that's important to me. ."Tell your message first showing much attention in your facial expression, and then repeat the same message with a blank look empty of any emotion. Ask your test subject to let you know which message evokes a more favorable response the other person would respond more favorably to which message? The messaging looks best to support the verbal communication with interested parties. Look no-expression is in contradiction with the post. You'll probably also note that each time, your voice sounds a little different from vibrant to monotonous. Your goal is in line with your message when you have your facial expressions firmly behind the message. And hold your chin up and get that face of yours alive when you're expressing your word.

- **GESTURES:** Gestures are what you do while you are communicating with your hands. I know those people who were told not to speak with their hands when they were younger. I, too, heard that message when I was a kid, wondering if something bad would happen if you were talking with your mouth. How unfair is it to use your hands to say something? Not one thing! In reality, if you use no movements at all when you talk, you're more dangerous (in terms of boring other people). Using gestures to come across assertively, help your message flow properly, and basically to punctuate or illustrate key points when you're talking. During informal and social interactions, people often do just that. Only add that same commitment to your critical work-related messages. You may also note that your movements contribute to your facial expressions, helping you convey your message within your own style in an animated manner. (The bone of the hand is linked to the bone of the face... Sing along, all now.)

AVOIDING BODY-LANGUAGE PITFALLS

Would you like to see your stance, facial expressions and movements as calm, animated and relaxed? I know you want

153

your posture, facial expressions, and gestures to come across as confident, animated, and relaxed however, other conducts make you less than assertive and generate emotions ranging from disinterest to disgust.

- **SLOUCHING:** Many office chairs are very comfortable, particularly the big cushy ones that you often see in the conference rooms. They encourage sitting back and relaxing. Unfortunately when you do that, irrespective of what kind of chair you're in, you find yourself too comfortable. More energy also gets behind your speech. Slouching was no good at the dinner table as you might have been told as a child. It's also no good if you want someone to interact assertively and be taken seriously.

- **INVADING SPACE:** This pitfall happens even more when people stand and try to engage in lively conversation. It's the place where you get too close to the other person for comfort. Certainly if that person is leaning away from you that is a sure sign that you have crossed the physical space comfort zone.

Chapter 15. Communication and Relationship

Excellent communication is a significant element of all affairs and is an important ingredient of any good relationship. Every affair has difficulties; however, good communication approaches might make it simple to handle disagreement and make a stronger relationship. People understand how vital interaction is, bar not what communication is and how people may apply excellent communication in their affairs. People regularly perplex communication for speaking or making discussion, and this is the reason why several of these persons are so unproductive when it comes to how to interact effectively. Communication in an affair, at its best, is about linking and applying your oral, printed, and physical abilities to accomplish your partner's desires. It is not concerning making tiny talk. It concerns understanding your partner's position; giving support and permitting your spouse to know that you are his or her admirer.

Before you struggle on developing your communication in an affair, you require understanding that not everybody has the similar communication inclinations. Several persons like to speak some desire touch while other people are visual or react better to present giving than an external conversation of thoughts. Everyone is inimitable and reacts to different motivations in different ways, and efficient interaction with your spouse shall come from accepting this. Your spouse might be telling you accurately what they require, however you have to be aware of how they express this message to you. If there is a lack of communication, you shall miss the chance to develop trust and confidence, and you shall both feel aggravated in the affair.

Be Available in your Affair

To develop communication in affairs and accurately realize what your spouse is communicating to you, be present. Set time away and give yourself a hundred per cent to converse with your spouse. He or she must truly feel that they have your undivided concentration and that he or she is your main concern. It is intricate to pay attention and be available, conscious, and attentive when you are annoyed and worried or are struggling with issues that need time far from your bond. This is a component of life; however, it is vital to understand that it is not a justification for abandoning communication in an affair. Keep in mind that closeness, love, and dependence are

156

developed when matters are complicated, not when they are simple. If we surrender at each mark of struggle, we could never develop and progress. Grab these chances to discover how to deal with disagreement and pressure in a healthy way and observe as you develop and thrive with your spouse.

Defy letting an easy conversation regarding what is happening currently decentralize into a repeat of every mistake that has ever occurred between you and your spouse. This is the reverse of caring and efficient communication in an affair. Instead, review the current circumstances and discover what you might do at this time. Pause and memorize why you are in the relationship and recall that your objective, the result that you cherish, is to reinforce your relationship, create intimacy, and find out how to talk better. How to converse effectively is more than expressing the correct feelings. You must also be attentive to body language. Someone might give all the caring and kind words in the world to your spouse, however, if your hands are folded on your upper body and you have a frown on your face, your spouse is unlikely to react positively. How to converse in an association implies paying attention, caring, and supporting your entire effort. Bend toward your spouse, keep your look calm and open, and tap him or her in a temperate manner. Prove to him or her through all your terms, deeds and expressions that you are his or her lover even if you are in disagreement.

Be Straightforward

Retreating from disagreement seems dishonestly secure and calm, however, it is no alternative for trust in an affair, and it shall never assist you to discover how to communicate effectively. Moving away from a fight is a momentary method of dealing with a constant communication concern and must be done for achieving a short cooling-down time. When you differ with your spouse, you must be capable of trusting that what you speak shall be heard and appreciated, and so does your spouse.

When you or your spouse are unenthusiastic to disagreement, you might get yourselves concealing your feelings to satisfy each other and evade troubles. This momentary mediation Band-Aid spins a collaborative affair into a one-way lane, and that is not a good result. The cheerfulness and closeness you used to have shall progressively wear away, and it shall take the association with it. On the other hand, instead of paying no attention to matters, it is vital that you both find out how to converse effectively to one another.

Effective Communication for Seduction

The work of seducing is a delicate and alluring entertainment, which entails using the correct quantity of display or camouflage, magnificent or revealing vaguely, stating something, but not revealing a lot. This discontinuous between an individual and the other plays a huge role in seductive communication in which the purpose to lessen the interpersonal space with hopes to enhance closeness is strongly tangled with the desire to save one's pride in case of dismissal. It also regards the preference of communicative deeds, which is deliberately allusive: to be competent, it must entail giving a clue of what is on display without illuminating too much. Simplicity and referential data are surely not the idiosyncratic aspects of seductive interaction; in fact, what appears to matter most is how the match is played, instead of the components of the match itself.

For this uniqueness, seductive contact stands out in its personal right as a tip of examination in communicative manners. Mainly it makes it probable to scrutinize the connections between diverse structures of expression and to explain some tactic of obliquity and camouflage skill, which are defined as miscommunication types.

Communication in Marriage

Good marriage flourishes on the free exchange of feeling, wishes, and ideas. In addition, interaction is one of the most significant features of an enjoyable marriage. Marriages experiences tough times, which might alter the manner spouses, converse with each other. Several partners grow bad behavior and create unhelpful patterns when matters are not working well. Excellent communication is the basis of a happy marriage. Several marriages can be saved if partners improved the manner, they talk to each other. It is frequently the simplest terrible behavior that gets partners into difficulty. When a marriage falls on a bumpy track, unconstructiveness develops. Troubles shoot up as both partners duplicate their fault repeatedly.

Shouting at your Partner

If you feel annoyed, you possibly begin raising your tone. Rage creates anxiety. As nervousness develops, you search for means of letting it go or saying it. Shouting at your partner becomes an immediate and easy choice, although it frequently causes more difficulty than help. It might be excellent to let loose your anxiety on your partner when he or she upset you, however, the sense of fulfilment is regularly transitory what you speak in your irritated condition is expected to add firewood to the bonfire.

Shouting unleashes many strong, unenthusiastic feelings. Regardless of the message, you are attempting to converse at that point, the feeling shall be the focal point.

It is not that you may not express several strong feelings when you talk. However, shouting goes past the contour. It makes the point for an exchange of intense sentiments rather than unmistakably communicated expressions. Even if your feeling is the information you want to share, an entirely sentimental exchange might easily change into a fatiguing, negative routine. At some position, feelings require to outbreak in a manner that lets you go past them, not stimulate them.

Allow your Expressions to Speak

If you might keep your feelings in check, your point might really go through. This does not imply you must attempt shoving your feelings out of the track. They might be a vital element of your circumstances. However, remember the entire purpose of communicating is to be unmistakably understood. To enable that, your path of communication should follow two ways. Extreme sentiment meddles with that. Take time by yourself to assist you to drive the wave of emotions and allow them to stay separately.

Another alternative is to take a swift work outbreak before you carry on the discussion. Exercise is a wonderful pressure reducer and it might easily divert you from your powerful feelings. It is hard to concentrate on your plight if you are almost out of breath. You might as well find it accommodating to note down the issues that you desire to state so you take care to convey your point noticeably. It is good to take time discussing a subject that makes you emotional. You shall solve the crisis effortlessly if you might keep your partner on your side rather than pushing him or her away.

Avoid Cutthroat Mind-set

You might have to be competitive in the game in some regions of your days, but your matrimony is not a completion. When one individual is constantly the conqueror, both partners lose. When you see yourself making a case in your brain with supporting evidence for every difference, you might triumph the disagreement each time. Nevertheless, you might do more to drain and dishearten your partner than something else.

The Desire to Succeed

An individual with emotional doubts might overcompensate by attempting to look greater than his or her partner attempts. If he or she stays successful, they feel better and more positive. They might have difficulty being susceptible, even with their partner. To do so could reveal their doubts. This could conflict with their trust that they are victorious. Does your partner exhaust of your success in dancing and you require to always having the final say? Perhaps they just desire you to go down. They are maybe better off to be next to you when you prove fault. You might not be used to your partner showing kindness toward you. When you married a good individual, you have nothing to worry about and everything to be happy. You do not have to be successful to feel happy.

Avoid being Self-centered

Have you constantly stopped paying attention to the talk going on in your brain? In most cases, it is centered on what you appear, how you muddled, and what you have on your timetable.

Logically, this talk is somewhat unfair because it is from your perception. Nevertheless, how about the talk that refers to your partner? Is it concerning how much enjoyment you shall have, what you anticipate from your lover, and what type of disposition you are experiencing?

Accept your Partner's Opinion

Kindness and understanding behaviors might go a long way toward fostering a good marriage. Instead of speculating if they shall ever fill the dishwasher correctly, do something you understand your partner shall value. When you maintain a model of being kind and considerate toward your partner, they will ultimately speak or do something as a reaction. They may hood their comments, as they do not recognize if this trend shall continue. They might be patient to see if this kindness is a publicity stunt or a set of fresh, positive routines. When they notice that you are real and constant with your hard work over time, your point shall be understandable. Allow those self-centered feelings pass by and continue doing adoring things for your partner. Additionally, you might not feel adoring at first if you do this kind of work. If your spouse does not speak something, you might question why you are struggling at all. The more you try with bigheartedness, the more you shall unsurprisingly feel kind and adoring toward your partner.

Chapter 16. How to Use Communication Skills for Business

Communication is an important part of all auspices in life. In business, it is a critical skill at all stages. Whether you are just starting the business or if you have been around for a while, effective communication is important to help you succeed.

Through the course of your career you have come across different people whose methods of communication vary from time to time. In each of your encounters, you must have realized the importance of getting your message across.

Effective communication will help you work smarter and get along better with your workmates. It is also important to establish stronger connections with your workmates and create an enabling business environment.

These are necessary if you are to have a healthy balance at work.

Written Communication at Work

The most common form of communication in any workplace is written communication. This particularly applies to formal interaction. You write emails, memos and so on.

Of course, you will still engage colleagues and clients through verbal communication, but written communication carries an official aspect to it.

One of the reasons why written communication is key in a formal setting is because it allows you to keep records. You will always have a record of emails sent and all correspondence with clients and your colleagues.

During official meetings, someone is appointed to write minutes which are filed for future reference.

For written communication an important skill you should master is how to argue your position amicably. More often you write reports, and other forms of communication where you are required to give your opinion on something.

For this purpose, try to use examples and specific data sets to help you communicate the desired message.

In a business setting, it is important to ensure that you keep all communication brief but as informative as possible.

You would not want to confuse the audience with unnecessary information that gets their attention from the important stuff.

Other than providing the necessary information, another important skill you should master in written communication is conducting follow-ups from time to time.

This is important in that it will help you make sure the recipient has all the information they need, and they understand what is required of them. Without feedback, you might not know whether they will respond accordingly until they do, which might be too late.

Conducting follow-ups is also important in the sense that it allows you to ensure that everyone who receives the communiqué is actively working towards meeting its prescribed goals.

Becoming an Active Listener

Every day we communicate with people at different levels. Taking an example of the workplace, you interact with junior and senior colleagues all the time. You also have colleagues who operate at your level that you consider your peers.

In human interaction, seniority levels usually influence the way we communicate from time to time. It creates a level of bias that affects communication.

It is important to ensure that everyone is on the same page, and in the presence of such biases, this becomes a problem. More often there is a predisposition in many businesses where senior employees and junior employees feel neither party listens to the other. Active listening is about more than just hearing what your colleagues are talking about, it is also about focusing on the emotions and intent behind the message.

Your views and opinions are not always the final say. This is one of the most important things you need to realize when listening to people in a conversation. Listening means you allow them to become part of the conversation too.

You consider their thoughts, opinions and expressions. You show them that their view of the problem or solution is being considered in the situation you are addressing.

The best thing about listening to people in the conversation is that they realize they are equally important, and feeling that they are involved in the process helps to create an amicable business environment. You should learn more than just how to listen to people, you need to learn how and when to pause in the conversation so that the audience can interject.

You also need to learn how to encourage them to participate by asking the right questions. The idea here is to help them engage and become a part of the conversation, not just passive listeners who might even be unwilling to be there in the first place.

Improving Verbal Communication

In the workplace we communicate through different ways. Most of the communication is written for formal reasons, but this should not take away the importance of effective verbal communication. You engage people all the time, so you should learn how to communicate with them too. Opinions, thoughts, ideas and updates are often communicated verbally.

This happens in official and unofficial meetings and gatherings.

Just in the same way that you emphasize clarity in written communication at work, the same applies to verbal communication. Your interaction needs to be specific and concise. There is so much information that people come across during the day that information overload is a common challenge in many workspaces. You should avoid adding to this burden by keeping conversations brief where necessary.

In light of recent technological advances, we encounter a lot of technological noise in the workplace, and as a result many people have a very short attention span.

This could also be influenced by other factors like deadlines they are working hard to beat, pressure from external and internal influences and so on.

Considering these influences, it is wise to ensure that verbal communication is handled in an appropriate manner.

The best thing about verbal communication at work is that it helps employees engage one another for mutual reasons. They can use this to clarify anything that they do not understand, seek permissions, and so on.

When handled properly, verbal communication offers the best support for written and other forms of communication and can help you make the workplace better and more accommodating for everyone.

Interpersonal Communication

Unless you work with robots, interpersonal communication skills are necessary in a business setting. These skills help you establish and foster strong relationships with your colleagues and other stakeholders in the business.

Interpersonal communication skills are also important to create an element of trust.

It is easier to relate to people that you trust than those you don't. The need for proper interpersonal communication skills is that they help in many cases where situations with employees might end up in a stalemate.

If you can engage one another, it is easier to find common ground by looking at alternative ways of handling issues.

Interpersonal communication skills are also necessary to create a sense of empathy in the business.

Given your interaction with your colleagues, you understand their perspective and what they are going through, so in many cases you will understand one another beyond the content of the conversation, guided by the underlying context.

In as much as you are operating in a business environment, interpersonal communication gives you the necessary skills to help you communicate and connect with one another at a personal level.

Business environments where quality interpersonal communication is present are usually accommodating and exciting for employees. People understand one another and go out of their way to help each other. This is also good for their overall well-being.

Conclusion

The value and importance of communication in the world today is more important than ever. As the influence of technology embeds deeper into our lives, it is increasingly crucial that we learn how to communicate with one another better and more efficiently.

Today there are many ways through which we can interact with one another. As a result, you come to realize that over time we spend less time on interpersonal communication, with most of our communication taking place over the internet through various devices and applications.

While technology is good for the future of mankind, the fact that most people are losing touch with basic communication skills is something that we need to look at.

From the beginning, we realize that communication must be about understanding one another. If you cannot understand each other, it is impossible to communicate effectively.

This is one of the reasons why you need to ensure you brush up on your communication skills. The good thing with communication skills is that each day is always a chance to learn something new.

There is no point to life when you say you have learned all there is to know about communication.

By interacting with different people all the time, you have a good chance of learning more about them from their experiences.

Our lives are essentially an aggregate of all experiences we have had and those we have shared with people around us. The same applies to communication.

As you interact with different people, you learn about their preferences, their reactions, and predispositions and with time you become considerate of their needs. This is all about empathy.

We get through the day by communicating with a lot of people. In traffic you have to communicate with other drivers or you risk causing an accident.

At work you must communicate instructions clearly in order to meet the overall objectives of the organization.

There is a lot of communication going on around you, and you need to learn how to improve your communication skills so that you become an active and engaging player in the communication dimensions you are a part of daily. As you go through this you realize that there are different scenarios that always demand a specific form of communication.

Written communication might be effective especially in terms of record keeping, but it is not effective all the time. There are moments where verbal communication will convey a message better than written communication. The secret, therefore, is to learn how to choose the appropriate form of communication through which you can communicate effectively and address your needs and the needs of the recipient.

While verbal and written communication is dominant in modern communication, you also learn the importance of body language and the use of visual aids in improving the quality of communication. These are learning points that will help you learn how to support whichever form of communication you use with others, and in the process communicate better with your audience.

Remember that the ultimate goal in quality communication is to ensure there is no room for ambiguity. We talk about effective communication all the time, but most of us never really pay attention to what it entails. As a result, we end up making mistakes in the course of communication, costly mistakes whose consequences are far-reaching.

While the core objective of this is to help you improve your communication skills, an important takeaway that you not miss is the importance of mutual understanding in communication. Why is this important? In as much as we believe we communicate by moving a message from one person to the other, it is also possible that no communication might have taken place.

Confusion especially arises when the audience cannot see the connection between the sentiments or feelings in the message and the context of the message. It also arises when your body language and spoken or written words are not in tandem.

As a good communicator, you need to learn how to align all the necessary elements together so that you do not create chaos in the recipient's mind, wherever you are, from what you have learned in here you should try to make sure that your communication is in such a manner that you can create easy understanding with the recipient.

There are many factors that influence the nature of communication and its effectiveness. The best you can do is to ensure that the factors that are within your control are properly aligned to ease the communication process. Besides, when the recipient understands you easily, you get the response you need with minimal fuss, which is a good thing, right?

Effective communication encompasses an aggregate of all forms of communication, from written to verbal and body language.

To become a good communicator, you have to learn how to harness all the above. It is important to learn all these forms of communication because this knowledge will help you determine the best approach to use when communicating with someone.

While all of the methods are effective in one way or another, you must always conduct a situational analysis to determine the best way to approach any situation. Learning to communicate effectively also involves awareness of the audience and their needs. Unfortunately, most people ignore the recipient all the time.

CPSIA information can be obtained
at www.ICGtesting.com
Printed in the USA
LVHW080921171220
674413LV00007B/202

9 781801 324960